EASY AIRBRUSH PROJECTS
for CRAFTERS &
DECORATIVE PAINTERS

D1303955

Purchased from
Multnomah County Library
Title Wave Used Bookstore
216 NE Knott St, Portland, OR
503-988-5021

EASY AIRBRUSH PROJECTS
for CRAFTERS &
DECORATIVE PAINTERS

LINDY BROWN

NORTH LIGHT BOOKS

Cincinnati, Ohio

Easy Airbrush Projects for Crafters & Decorative Painters. Copyright © 1997 by Lindy Brown. Printed and bound in China. All rights reserved. No part of this book may be reproduced in any form or by any electronic or mechanical means including information storage and retrieval systems without permission in writing from the publisher, except by a reviewer, who may quote brief passages in a review. Published by North Light Books, an imprint of F&W Publications, Inc., 1507 Dana Avenue, Cincinnati, Ohio 45207. (800) 289-0963. First edition.

Other fine North Light Books are available from your local bookstore, art supply store or direct from the publisher.

01 00 99 98 97   5 4 3 2 1

Library of Congress Cataloging-in-Publication Data

Brown, Lindy.
    Easy airbrush projects for crafters and decorative painters / by Lindy Brown.
      p. cm.
    Includes index.
    ISBN 0-89134-746-1 (pbk. : alk. paper)
    1. Painting. 2. Airbrush art. 3. Handicraft. 4. Decoration and ornament. I. Title.
TT385.B76   1997
745.7'23—DC21   96-54738
                                                       CIP

Edited by Kathy Kipp and Dawn Korth
Production edited by Bob Beckstead
Interior designed by Clare Finney
Cover designed by Brian Roeth

North Light Books are available for sales promotions, premiums and fund-raising use. Special editions or book excerpts can also be created to specification. For details, contact: Special Sales Manager, F&W Publications, 1507 Dana Avenue, Cincinnati, Ohio 45207.

Dedication

To my four daughters, who always understood when Mom was "out of town!"—Retta, Jan, Susie and Anna. Love you, Mom.

Acknowledgments

To my teacher Cindy McCown, who said the technique of teaching airbrushing was possible. To Mollie Perry, who team coaches with me. And to Jean Zawicki for sharing her "Rose" pattern and Eleanor Zimmerman for sharing her "Old-Fashioned Girl" pattern. These two ladies are outstanding members of the Society of Decorative Painters. Their permission to use their patterns to show design adaptation to airbrush opens a whole world of patterns available to the "decorative airbrusher"!

Table of Contents

Dear Decorative Painter,

This book is an exciting way to greet you and introduce you to my way of decorative painting with an airbrush. So many new techniques and special looks the airbrush can give to your art and craft work could begin here. I have tried to lift the "mystery" of airbrushing and show you how easy it can be in step-by-step basic lessons. The projects in this book will cover many techniques and uncover answers to some of the "how did they do that?" queries about airbrushing. The tools you will find the easiest to use are frisket films and a cutting knife. The way they are used to make airbrushing simple will surprise you.

The interaction of opaque and transparent colors is even more dramatic when you mix color right on the painting surface as you airbrush. The look of airbrushed artwork will add a new dimension to the way you paint and the way you look at patterns and designs. Many times the finishing details are done with a liner brush, felt-tip pen or colored pencils, the main color and design being laid in with airbrush and friskets. Precut stencils are a natural with the airbrush. Edges are easy to maintain and the gradation of color is controlled with a tip of the finger on the dual-action trigger of an airbrush.

The secret of airbrushing is keeping the airbrush in condition as you paint and cleaning it well before you put it away. There is no magic here, just the attention all brushes demand, hand or air.

For myself, this book has been a great experience, planning and executing the lessons from the simplest to the complex and introducing you to my favorite art form. If you haven't heard about the Society of Decorative Painters (393 N. McLean Blvd., Wichita, KS 67203-5968) or the Stencil Artisans League, Inc. (P.O. Box 920190, Norcross, GA 30092), they are a great, creative and sharing bunch of people. Membership in either or both of these societies will introduce you to many friends who, like you, love to paint.

I wish you excitement and great paintings with the airbrush.

Best,

Lindy B.

PART ONE

GETTING STARTED

Airbrushes

SINGLE-ACTION AIRBRUSHES

This basic style of airbrush consists of a jar with an air nozzle aimed at an external tip. Most companies refer to it as a "gun" or a "sprayer," and market it to hobby customers. Applications are limited for this kind of airbrush because it is not extremely versatile. Only a small amount of adjustment is possible by turning the paint tip to raise or lower it. This affects the siphon action lifting the paint to the tip as the air is blowing across the top of the opening, but it doesn't affect the amount of air used. The resulting spray pattern is coarse, so this is a great way to cover a surface with a lot of paint in a short time. The Visions AirPainter, which uses special acrylic-based paints in bottles with "quick connect" caps, allows a separate air source unit to be transferred from bottle to bottle with no mixture of color. This tool for air-projected paint is my choice for basecoating surfaces with paint, for antiquing large pieces and for spraying varnish.

There are several single-action, internal-mix airbrushes on the market that are more readily adjustable to paint volume and spray pattern. They produce a finer spray when pre-adjusted by the operator to the desired size and volume of paint. When the trigger is depressed, the air and paint combine internally to create the spray pattern.

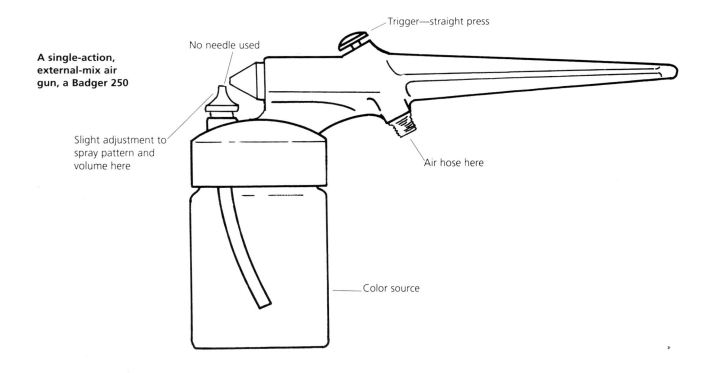

Trigger—straight press

No needle used

A single-action, external-mix air gun, a Badger 250

Slight adjustment to spray pattern and volume here

Air hose here

Color source

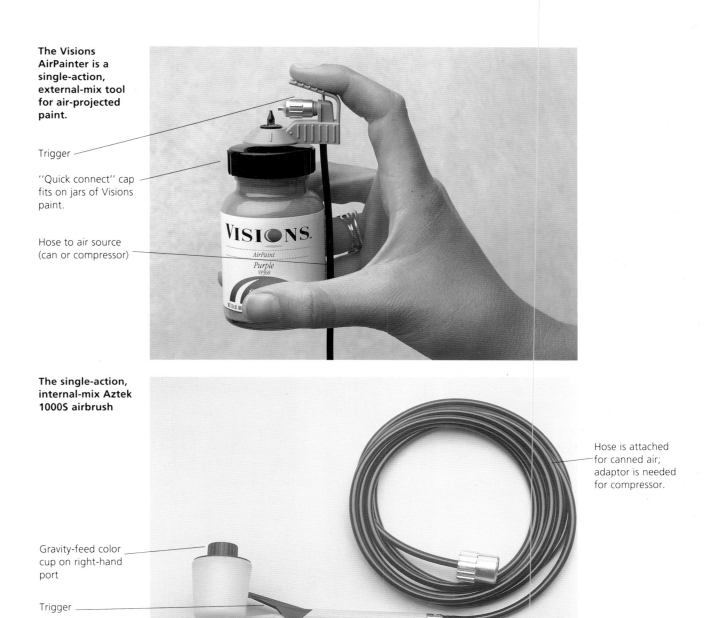

The Visions AirPainter is a single-action, external-mix tool for air-projected paint.

Trigger

"Quick connect" cap fits on jars of Visions paint.

Hose to air source (can or compressor)

The single-action, internal-mix Aztek 1000S airbrush

Hose is attached for canned air; adaptor is needed for compressor.

Gravity-feed color cup on right-hand port

Trigger

Adjust color spray here.

DUAL-ACTION AIRBRUSHES

The double- or dual-action airbrush has a trigger to control the volume of both air and paint. When the trigger is depressed the air flows through the airbrush and out the nozzle or tip. When the air is engaged and the trigger is pulled back, the needle retracts in the tip of the airbrush and allows the paint to flow through the opening. Controlling the amount of air and paint requires the dual actions, that is pressing down and pulling back the trigger. Since this takes practice, most airbrushes will have practice lessons included in the instructions.

All metal airbrushes require at least partial disassembly for cleaning and light maintenance. It is important to retain the schematics for your own information in reassembling the airbrush after cleaning; and if you need replacement parts you will have the parts numbers readily available. Maintenance requires removing and cleaning the needle and the tip after a day of airbrushing.

My preference for a dual-action airbrush is the Aztek 3000S, which has all types of color cup styles available, as well as a simple cleaning procedure to keep me painting. It is made of a lightweight, high-impact resin

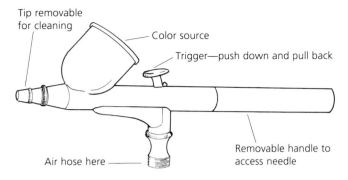

Tip removable for cleaning
Color source
Trigger—push down and pull back
Air hose here
Removable handle to access needle

The Iwata HPC is a dual-action airbrush with a fixed gravity feed.

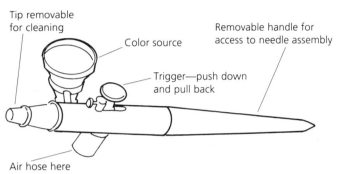

Tip removable for cleaning
Color source
Removable handle for access to needle assembly
Trigger—push down and pull back
Air hose here

Thayer Chandler A, a double-action, internal-mix airbrush

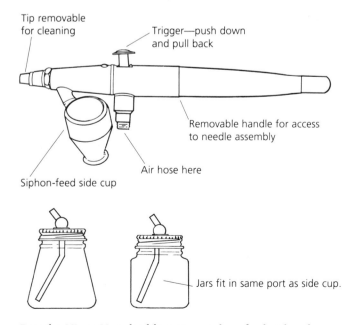

Tip removable for cleaning
Trigger—push down and pull back
Removable handle for access to needle assembly
Air hose here
Siphon-feed side cup
Jars fit in same port as side cup.

Paasche VL or V, a double-action siphon-feed airbrush

and the tip and needle are all in one unit. Removing the color source and running a cleaner through the tip is considered "light" maintenance. Removing the tip and lightly brushing both ends with a child's toothbrush usually cleans it. If the tip or nozzle of an airbrush has been standing with paint (especially acrylic-based paint) for some time and these procedures do not clean it, I use a glass of hot water and a tablet designed for cleaning false teeth to soak the nozzle for about twenty minutes. I rinse it in hot water, scrub with the brush, and I'm ready to go again.

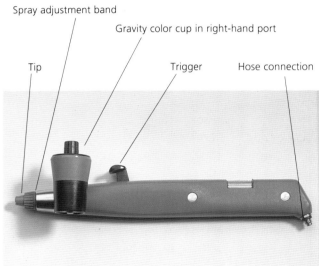

Spray adjustment band
Gravity color cup in right-hand port
Tip
Trigger
Hose connection

The Aztek 3000S is my personal choice for a dual-action airbrush.

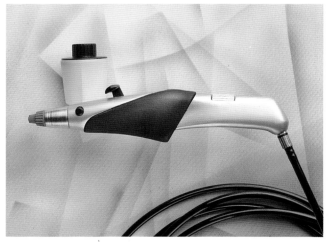

The Aztek A470, pictured here, is the very newest in dual-action airbrushes.

Air Sources

Your air source can be as simple as an adaptor unit and canned air. As you use up the air, the can cools down and your air pressure will diminish. If you let the can warm up to room temperature, you will again have the pressure you need. This is an inexpensive way to try air-projected painting, but to develop skill and master airbrushing techniques you'll need a dual-action airbrush and a constant air source.

A hobby-sized compressor without a holding tank can operate one airbrush well. It produces a slight pulsation to the spray that will appear in detail or small spray patterns. This is because it is a diaphragm-style compressor. Be sure it can operate at 25 to 35 pounds per square inch (psi) (1.9 Bar to 2.7 Bar). And no, a small compressor that is used for inflating car tires does *not* work!

A large compressor with a holding tank can usually operate more than one airbrush at a time. The more air used, the more often it will turn on to maintain a constant pressure in the tank. A moisture trap is important to prevent condensation from the holding tank from coming through the hose and onto your surface. Again, 25 to 35 pounds psi (1.9 Bar to 2.7 Bar) is the recommended pressure. Compressors can be found wherever airbrushes are sold.

A carbon dioxide tank is great. It's quiet, capable of delivering 25 to 35 pounds psi (1.9 Bar to 2.7 Bar), and is a good source of air. This is especially true where noise is a problem and the expense of a silent compressor is beyond the budget. The main pressure gauge will tell you when a refill is necessary. About every fourth refill it will be tested to comply with local safety standards. Since these vary from community to community, contact a compressed air company where you live. Sometimes you can lease tanks and pay for the refills and maintenance. It pays to shop around.

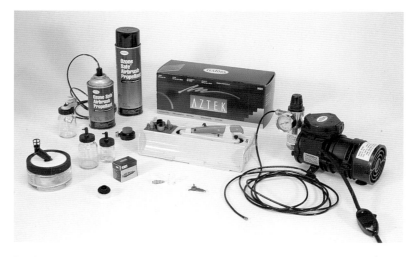

The small diaphragm compressor at the far right produces about 25 to 35 pounds psi (1.9 Bar to 2.7 Bar). Large and small cans of air are on the upper left. The smaller can is connected to an AirPainter attached to an empty 2-ounce (56.8ml) bottle. Also pictured is a complete setup for airbrushing, including the airbrush, various nozzles and color sources, a regulator for attaching to canned air and a cleaning station.

This metal Eclipse airbrush by Iwata is connected to the small diaphragm compressor with a braided hose recommended by the manufacturer. Also pictured is a regulator for attaching to canned air. In the foreground an Eclipse is dismantled to show the parts, including the handle and the needle below it.

Paints

Paints, dyes and other coatings designed for airbrush use will have that designation on the label. Some examples are Visions by Testor Corp., ComArt by Medea and Deka Perm Air. Be sure to read the label and understand the toxicity. Wearing a face mask or respirator is important when using air-projected paint.

Paint designed for airbrush use will be of light viscosity but have a heavily pigmented base. It will cost more per ounce than most craft paints but will go two to three times farther in usage.

Airbrush-designed acrylics and some model paints have great coverage. The colors are clean and easily mixed to tint and shade. Since most airbrushers mix colors on the painted surface, the clarity of color is especially important.

Matching the paint to the surface you are airbrushing is vital for success. Many inks and watercolors do not do well beyond papers, and some acrylics do not have the correct viscosity for use on papers. *Read the labels* and test.

Using heavy paints not designed for airbrushing is not always successful because watering them down to a usable consistency may water down the color as well.

The best paints to adjust to airbrushing consistency are labeled "concentrated" and have a flat or matte finish. Liquitex Concentrated Artist Colors and Jo Sonja's Acrylics have this pigmentation and work very well. When diluting, I use equal parts paint and distilled water. I continue to add water a little at a time if this mixture does not go easily through the airbrush. The distilled water allows me to mix and store the colors on the shelf for later use without having to worry about bacteria forming in the mix. Also, Liquitex has a product called Flow-Aid. This is a water tension reducer, and mixed with water makes the mixing smoother and easier. Stirring as well as shaking is advised for smooth paint. And a word of advice—mark the bottles with brand, color and date.

Many craft paints work, and my suggestion is to try it if you have it on hand. The very fine particles in the "jewel" or iridescent colors work best from a gravity feed cup in small amounts. Between fillings of the cup, agitate the mix to keep the particles moving and suspended. The on/off of the trigger helps keep the particles moving as well. But watch the tip. It will tend to clog easier, so keep your cleaning brush nearby.

Projects in this book were painted with these paints, including Liquitex Concentrated Artist Colors, Visions, ComArt Primary color set, Jo Sonja's tube colors and Liquitex Wood Stain. Also pictured is Liquitex Flow-Aid for mixing with water to formulate color for the airbrush.

Besides paints, some other supplies used for the projects in this book are shown here. The Tracer is a projector used for enlarging from the Artograph Company. Matte finish Krylon Spray can be used to protect the fine layers of airbrush color between colors or before varnishing. Use Model Master clear coat finish over paintings on plastic or acrylic surfaces. At the far left are a plastic box from The Beadery "Adorables" and a brass stencil.

Surfaces

The projects in this book are done mostly on wood items and are directed to the decorative painter and crafter. Each project will explain the preparation of the wood piece featured. Many of these designs could be adapted to paper, painting boards or even to canvas.

If you are painting on tin, be sure to clean off all labels. Wash the piece with warm soapy water and rinse with vinegar and water (a fifty-fifty mix) to remove the residue of soap and oils. Do not handle the piece with bare hands after you wash it. For basecoating this surface I generally use a model or hobby paint with a flat or matte finish. I use acrylics over this surface for design, and a gloss varnish or overcoat. If you are using a stencil on a metal surface, small magnets will hold your stencil in place, leaving no sticky residue.

There are some plastics and acrylics available in craft and home decor stores that look great airbrushed. I prepare the surface the same way I do tin, and use the same kind of paints. My favorites are Testor's Accu-Flex and the Pactra Enamels with flat finish. If this is your choice, I suggest you also purchase the recommended cleaner, and that you use the finish designed for a plastic surface. I've had good luck painting plastic boxes and acrylic surfaces with this formula. Allow all painted surfaces a good drying and cure time, at least thirty-six hours before adding the final finish.

MISCELLANEOUS SUPPLIES

You will collect a variety of supplies as your airbrushing skills develop. Here are some I use and keep on hand.

- *Aztek Masking Film:* a frisket in a matte finish, available at craft and art stores and through mail order.
- *Duralene by Seth Cole:* I use this for a stencil film as it has a vellum finish on both sides and is very flexible but strong. You could also use a light mylar or acetate to make permanent stencils to keep. For one-time use on simple projects, I use papers of parchment weight.
- *Scotch 3M Long-Mask Masking Tape:* This blue, reusable tape doesn't leave a residue on the surface when removed and doesn't lift paint. It can be found in paint departments of hardware and home improvement stores.
- I always keep a no. 1 liner brush handy for painting fine detail, and an old toothbrush for scrubbing the tip of the airbrush when it gets plugged up with paint.
- I use Sakura Micron pens (.001mm) and their Identi-Pen for marking and drawing permanent lines for patterns.
- My favorite colored pencils are Liquitex Basics, with their soft, wide, strong-colored leads. I always sharpen them with a hand sharpener.

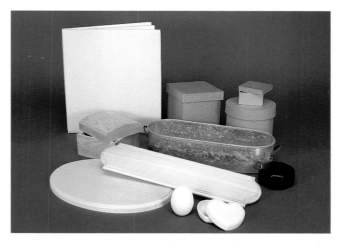
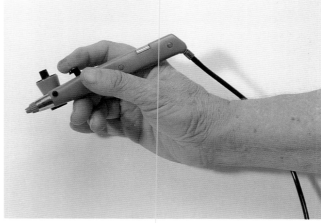

You can airbrush all kinds of objects and surfaces—just be sure to select the correct paint for the surface you're using, and be sure to hold your airbrush correctly. Hold it much like a pencil with your index finger on the trigger. Hold a metal airbrush with the thumb, middle and ring fingers around the valve core where the hose is attached to provide balance and control.

PART TWO

Basic Techniques

Veining Leaves

Adding the veins to leaves is a simple detail, made simpler by using a heart-shaped template. Yet this easy technique will add dimension and depth to your designs and make your leaves look more realistic.

The technique I show involves doing the leaf veining when you're base shading and highlighting, before you add the basic leaf color. However, you can switch the order if necessary and do the color glazing first. The veining is then done as an overlay color. The result is acceptable this way, but you should be aware that the colors do not meld as naturally as they do when you start with the veining.

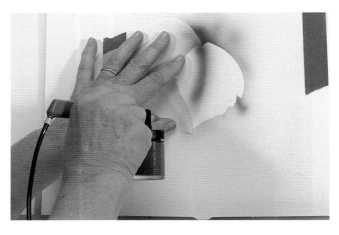
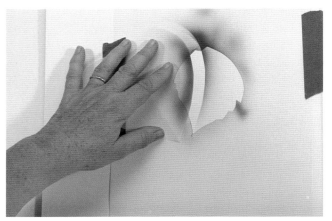

1 Start with whatever shading color you're using for your project. Place the heart template so the long curve on the side of the heart reaches from the base of the leaf to the tip. Airbrush along the curve, straddling the edge with color. Start from the base and move almost to the tip. If you paint the vein all the way to the tip of the leaf, it will have a stiff look. The leaf is more realistic with the main vein fading from the tip.

 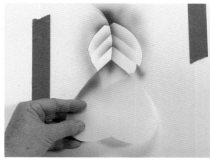 

2 To create the secondary veins branching off from the center vein, use the pointed tip of the heart template. Start at the base again and move toward the tip. Place the tip of the heart on the center vein and paint the secondary veins by aiming the airbrush at the tip of the leaf. Keep the distance between the vein lines as even as you can and allow the veins closest to the tip to be lighter. Don't allow the secondary veins to extend as far as the outer edge of the leaf to keep it from looking stiff.

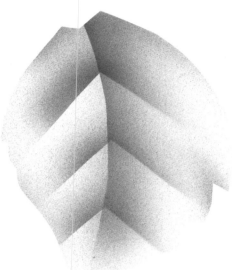

3 After the veins are underpainted, the next step is color glazing. Do this with an even, light coat of green, moving back and forth across the open area of the stencil or frisket. When you remove the stencil or frisket notice the sharp or "hard" edges of the leaf and the "soft" edges of the veining. The leaf veining and color all meld to create a softly curved leaf with natural looking veins. Check out "Ivy Key Holder" (page 30) and "Faux Finishes: Granite Box" (page 80) to see how to apply this technique to your projects.

Raindrop/Dewdrop

Use raindrops and dewdrops for accent and effect. Raindrops need a blue base color. You could scatter raindrops of different sizes all over a blue silk scarf or umbrella. Dewdrops can be placed on any color, so you can use dewdrops on leaves, floral petals, fruit, blades of grass or any other natural subject.

You need only two colors for the drop itself: White and Black (or a blue-black). You also need a template. I cut mine in many sizes from Duralene stencil film. Here's the technique you can use:

  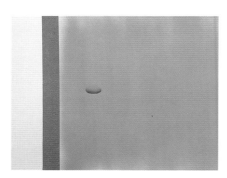

1 Determine where the finished raindrop is to be placed. Put the template on the design where you want the drop to be; then lower it ⅛ inch (0.3cm), and move it to the left ⅛ inch (0.3cm). Tape it in place.

2 With Black, airbrush along the lower and left edge of the open area. You are painting in a black shadow that occurs on the surface below the drop. You should be close to the surface and using a small spray pattern. Allow it to dry.

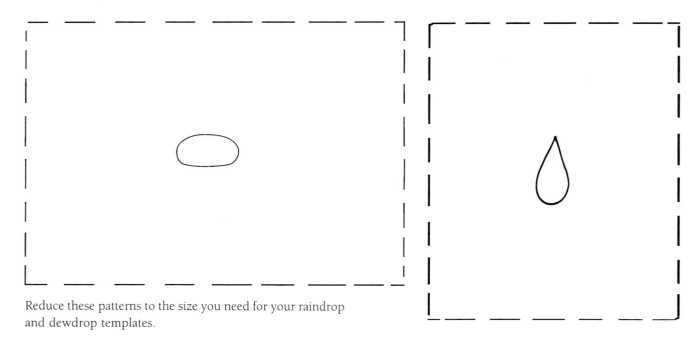

Reduce these patterns to the size you need for your raindrop and dewdrop templates.

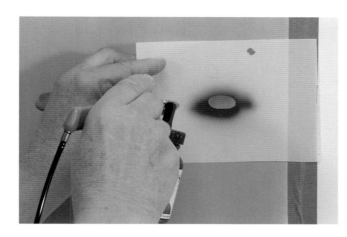 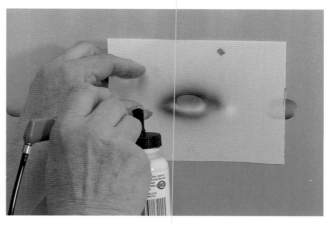

3 Move the template back to the original design position —up ⅛ inch (0.3cm) and to the right ⅛ inch (0.3cm)—and tape it in place. With a lighter spray pattern, airbrush the top and left edge of the open area of the template. You are using Black very sparingly, to achieve just a gray tint. Allow the paint to dry, and clean the airbrush.

4 Using White, accent the lower and right-hand area of the drop. The color should be strong at the bottom edge of the template and fade into the base-color area above.

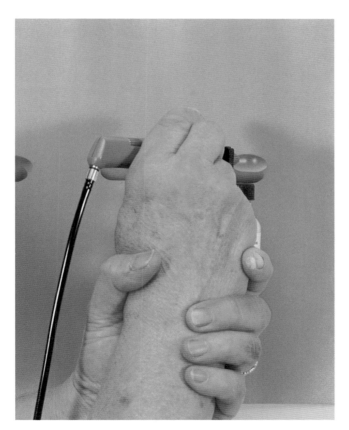

5 Set the airbrush to a fine spray pattern—just a line. Holding the airbrush about ¼ inch (0.6cm) from the surface, make a dot of White in the gray area on the upper right. Move your hand and make a short streak, not quite touching the dot, the same distance from the top edge of the raindrop. As you practice, allow this short streak to fade slightly.

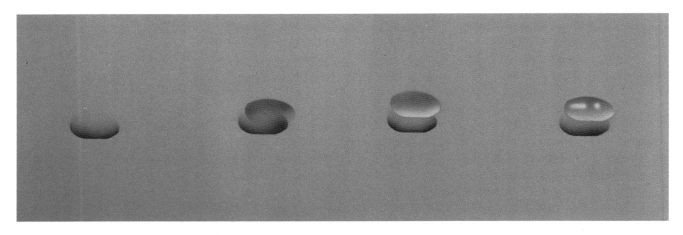

6 Here are the raindrop steps in sequence—shadow, gray, white, highlight.

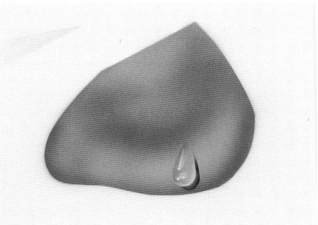

8 There you are—one of the great airbrush secrets! And did you ever imagine it could be so easy?

7 The technique for the dewdrop is the same, though you'll use a different shape for your template. You'll highlight where the drop is the heaviest in width, and on the bottom left side.

Antiquing

Decorative painters are familiar with antiquing because it's a common technique. But using the airbrush means your antiquing is easier than ever, and it looks great. Use this technique to "age" a finished piece, or simply to accent the contours. The effect you achieve depends on the colors you select.

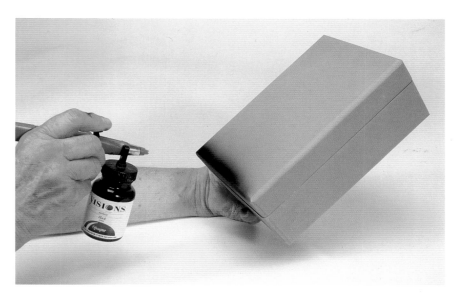

1 Use a color that contrasts with the base color. Aim the brush at a 45-degree angle to the edge of the box.

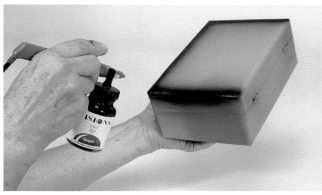

2 Spray, allowing both sides of the piece to be painted at the same time. A feathering or fading effect is created on both sides. If you practice on cardboard boxes to achieve the correct angle you will have more confidence when you antique wood items.

3 This piece shows extreme color contrast—much more stark than you would use, but it clearly illustrates the technique. A Burnt Umber over a light pine would be antiqued the same way, but the contrast would be much more subtle. Examples of antiquing are shown in the projects "Old-Fashioned Girl," "Candleglow Cabinet" and "Ivy Key Holder."

Starburst

Use a starburst to add sparkle to your airbrush designs. They're perfect as accents or to "pop a highlight" on bright, shiny subjects such as the Holiday Ornament (see page 70). You can also "bump" or increase the highlights on a dewdrop, or create stars in outer space. You'll need only a simple template and white paint. Usually, you'll make starbursts on a dark or medium color background.

1 Make a stencil by cutting a slot out of stencil film. I usually use a sheet about 4″×5″ (10.2cm×12.7cm). Make the two long cuts first, and then the two short ones. (As a shortcut, make several templates at a time with slots of varying widths and lengths to have on hand.)

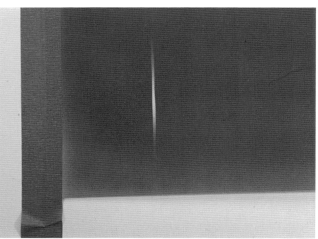

2 Position the slot vertically on the painting surface. Airbrush one burst from about 2 inches (5.1cm) without moving the airbrush. Aim at the center of the slot. Allow the color to dry.

3 Reposition the template with the slot sideways across the first line you painted. Aim at the center of the slot. Airbrush one burst of color similar to the previous one. Remove the template.

4 With the airbrush steady, aim at the center where the lines cross and lightly airbrush a faint, soft circle.

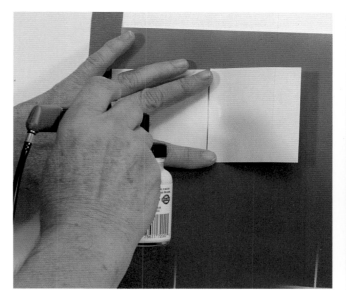

5 Once you gain confidence in your starburst technique you can even use repositionable notepapers to create the slots you need instead of using a template. After one or two stickdowns on fresh paint, however, the papers will lose their stickiness. So if you're doing more than one starburst you'll probably want to use a reusable template.

6 If you want to create the look of a corona or halo around the starburst, place a circle mask in the center and lightly airbrush around the outer edge. Here I'm using a jar lid, but anything round and not too big will do.

7 To create a small cluster of stars, hold the airbrush very close to the surface—½ inch (1.3cm) or closer if necessary. Airbrush a short burst of color to make a small dot. Do several dots in different sizes. Use the slot template vertically over a couple of the larger dots to create the effect of twinkling.

Use this slot template for your starbursts, or make the size you need.

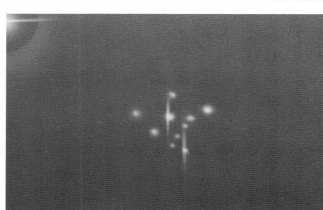

This is Ted E. Bear and he has a twinkle in his eye. This gives him a very mischievous look, and the smile plus the small sparkle on his nose help create the feeling he is putting something over on you.

The starburst is very effective in faces and will change the look or feel. A single starburst in only one eye, but echoed in the second eye with just a white dot, gives the feeling of impishness. If you put the starburst in both eyes, you will have an astonished look on the same face. You can emphasize a smile by putting a starburst on a tooth. A large devilish grin with lots of teeth and a starburst, as used in cartooning, will give the look of cunning.

Try a starburst on a dewdrop or raindrop or other sparkly surface, like a diamond. Use it as an accent when you are painting glass or other reflective surfaces, and to draw the eye to a focal point of the painting.

Creating a Stencil

In the art of airbrushing there are two basic looks: hard edge and soft edge. The hard edge is created with a stencil, frisket or material such as tape, applied firmly to the surface. Airbrushing along the edges of this applied masking leaves a sharp or hard edge when the stencil material is removed. A soft edge is a design edge with a fuzzy look where color fades. This is done with a handheld or loose template that allows the paint to drift slightly under the edge. Of course, with airbrushing there is always freehanding. This takes practice and drawing skill as well as airbrush knowledge and technique. Your confidence for airbrushing freehand will grow with practice.

Most beginning airbrushers depend on design technique using stencils or masked-off areas. The stencil part with open areas is called the positive. The cutout pieces removed from the background are referred to as the negative. If you apply these cutouts to a surface and airbrush around them you create the negative or background of the design area. When you remove the cutouts the image remains on the surface. This is a great way to paint florals and lace doilies.

Create a stencil for a design first by tracing it with simple lines. Decide at this point whether it is necessary to enlarge or reduce the design. You can use a projector for this process. I have a Tracer and find it easy to use and handy. A copy machine is OK, but often there are limitations in sizes that are available. Sometimes you'll need to size an image precisely to your painting surface, and I think nothing beats the projector method for that. I make several line drawings at a time of the size I want for a stencil.

Once you have traced your design and have several copies, study the image and realize that each element must be cut and removed without touching another on the same line. Dissect the design and begin to color elements that are not touching. Use a marker or colored pencil in a shade not related to the subject.

Restudy the drawing, select elements for a second layer and color them a different color. These elements can touch ones you previously colored, but they can't touch each other. The idea is to have no two elements of the same color touching. Repeat this process for as many layers as the stencil requires. This design required four, but could have taken as many as eight or nine layers, if I also took into account the convenience of applying the different colors as I separated elements.

Take as many layers of stencil film as you need, line them up and punch a hole in all four corners, or cut a diagonal slice off each corner. This will be your register device in addition to the design itself. On the first layer, line up your register with your drawing, mark it with pencil and secure the stencil with tape. Trace the areas to be cut out with red and outline the rest of the design in black.

Repeat the last step for as many layers as you have planned. When you have traced each layer with cutout areas in red and outlines in black, hold all the sheets up to a light source and check the design.

Cut out the red areas on each layer, carefully following the lines. Check frequently by holding the layers up to a light source. If they look good, and no corrections are needed, you are ready to proof. I use Scotch 3M Long-Mask Masking Tape for placing the proof on a paper surface. When you proof your design you will have a positive to file with your stencil. Make sure you spray the painted paper with a clear varnish, however, to protect the paint.

There is an organization made up of stencilers called the Stencil Artisans League, Inc. (P.O. Box 920190, Norcross, GA 30092). The dues of $30 per year will get you a membership, convention news and an *Artistic Stenciler Newsletter* subscription. They also have a chapter on the Internet. There are some awesome stencils available through this network. Some are nine or more layers and precut with a laser. I own a bunch!

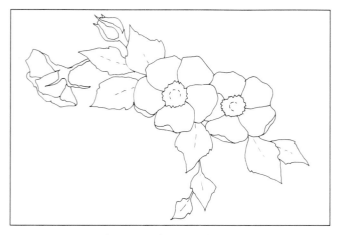

To create a stencil, start with a simple drawing.

Study the drawing and begin to isolate elements that do not touch each other on the same line. Color the elements with colored pencils. The idea is to have no two elements of the same color touching.

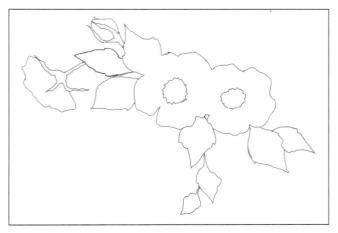

For each layer, take a sheet of stencil film and trace the areas to be cut out with red. Outline the rest of the design with black. This is the first layer.

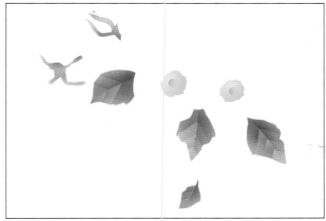

The proof of this layer shows how it is used. Airbrush the centers of the flowers with Yellow Ochre (from ComArt Opaque colors, the Primary set). Shade and vein the leaves with Ultramarine Blue, and glaze them with Chrome Green (also ComArt Opaque colors).

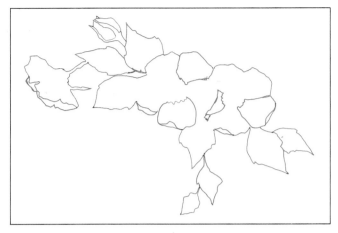

The second layer stencil looks like this. Notice how the areas colored purple on the reference drawing are marked with red to be cut out.

Paint the leaves in this layer in the same way as the previous layer. Use ComArt Opaque Orange lightly on the petals, deepening the color in the shade areas and where petals overlap.

The third layer stencil ready to cut.

Paint the leaves and petals in the layer with the same colors as the previous two layers.

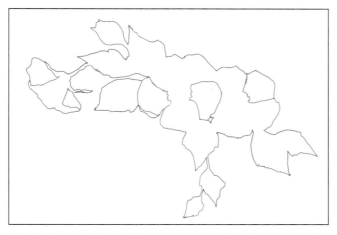

The final stencil layer. These areas are colored green on the reference drawing.

Complete the Wild Roses painting by finishing the remaining petals. When the paint dries, dip a toothpick in ComArt Opaque Yellow and Sienna Brown and make dots around the centers of the flowers. Use a fine-tip black pen for the small black marks.

Once you create a stencil you can use it over and over on many different surfaces. I used the Wild Roses on a wood slice. You might use pale pink for the roses and paint them on a papier-mâché keepsake box, or even on fabric.

Ivy Key Holder

In this project you will use a single-layer stencil to paint a perfect shadow. This easy, fun technique creates a polished three-dimensional look. You will also use a handheld heart-shaped template for veining leaves.

SUPPLIES

- **Signboard from Walnut Hollow stained with Light Oak waterbased wood stain, any brand (I used Visions).**
- **Ivy stencil from American Traditional Stencils #BL-576**
- **Visions Opaques colors: Burnt Umber, Holiday Green and Butter Yellow**
- **Scotch 3M Long-Mask Masking Tape**
- **Pencil, sanding pad and any brand of varnish.**

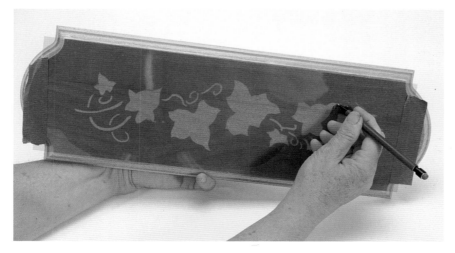

1 Place the stencil in position and tape the edges with masking tape. Mark with pencil the upper-right side of each large leaf. This will give you a register mark to realign the stencil after the shadow is painted.

2 Loosen the tape and move the stencil ¼ inch (0.6cm) down, and ¼ inch (0.6cm) to the left. Then reattach it firmly with masking tape at each end. With the airbrush 2 to 3 inches (5.1 to 7.6cm) from the surface, paint shadows with Burnt Umber along the top, bottom and left side of the leaves. Also paint the stems. Remove the stencil.

NOTE: When painting with the airbrush, always straddle the edge of the stencil with the paint and outline each section before moving into the open space. This will help keep the stencil in place and give a "hard edge" to the design.

3 Airbrush the edges of the board from a 45-degree angle using Burnt Umber. Be sure to cover all of the edge, allowing a soft spray to drift onto the surface of the board. This will give the key holder an antiqued look. Allow the board to dry completely before moving on.

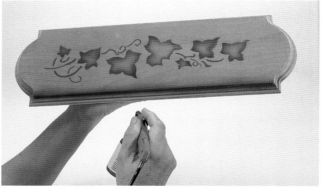

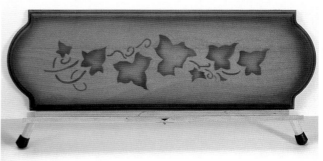

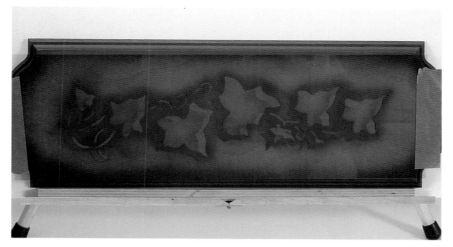

4 Replace the stencil in the original position using the pencil marks you made in the leaves. Tape the stencil securely; then airbrush the open areas with Holiday Green.

NOTE: Do not worry about the shadow lines that show through. Highlights will cover them.

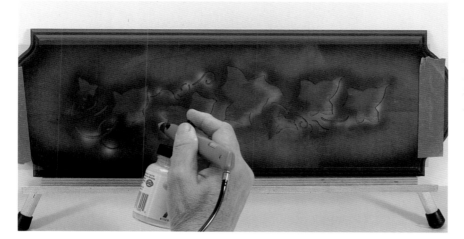

5 With Butter Yellow, airbrush along the left side and bottom of each leaf. The yellow color should cover the shadow lines that show through the green. Highlight the stems where shadow lines show through the green as well.

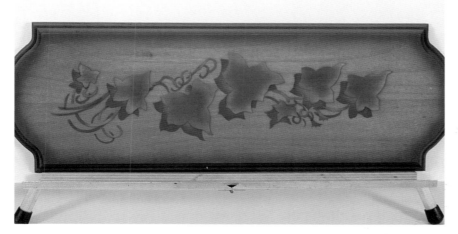

6 Here I've removed the stencil to show better where the highlights are placed. *Do not* remove your stencil while work is in progress!

7 Using a heart-shaped template, airbrush a vein through the center of each leaf with yellow. Then place the tip of the heart pointing toward the base of the leaf. Airbrush each side of the heart, forming lines that go from the center base to the top edge. (For more on veining leaves, see pages 16-17.) Allow the board to dry.

8 Remove the stencil and apply several coats of waterbased varnish.

9 For the key hooks, pencil dots from the center of the board out, spacing them evenly. Make a hole on each dot with a small nail. Remove the nail and screw in cup hooks by hand.

Use this heart-shaped template for veining the leaves.

Heart and Ribbons Pegged Board

Many stencils are separated into layers according to the colors used. Some are layered to allow the design to meet color on color without bridges between the cuts. That's the case with this 3-layer stencil. You'll paint a complex array of ribbons and flowers around the central heart without bridges between color sections. Each layer requires the use of four or more colors before the next stencil is placed.

While at first glance this project may seem complicated, the finished piece is well worth your time. So don't be intimidated.

SUPPLIES

- **Wood piece approximately 25″ × 11½″ (63.5cm × 29.2cm) (from Frank Tucker, Woodworker) and 6 pegs**
- **3-layer stencil from American Traditional Stencils #CDS-19**
- **Liquitex Concentrated Artist Colors: Hibiscus, Light Blue Violet, Dark Victorian Rose, Hooker's Permanent Green Hue, Baltic Green, Raw Sienna**
- **Sponge brush, soft cloth and Liquitex wood stain in Whitewash**
- **Pencil, Scotch 3M Long-Mask Masking Tape**

1 Examine the stencils. Note that they are numbered in the sequence they are to be used for developing the design. With a sponge or sponge brush apply Whitewash stain to the wood, moving in the direction of the grain. Stain the pegs also. Wipe off the excess stain with the soft cloth.

2 Place stencil layer no. 3 on the wood surface and center the large heart part of the design. Secure the stencil at each end with masking tape. Mark with pencil the triangle-shaped register marks on all four corners, then remove the stencil.

NOTE: The third stencil layer is used to set the register marks because the heart is the largest section in the design, and the focal point. This has to be centered first.

3 Match the register marks on stencil layer no. 1 and secure the stencil to the wood with masking tape. Begin painting the ribbon with Hibiscus. Airbrush the shaded areas first. Allow the color to fade by pulling back from the surface as you paint toward the highlight area. The motion is back and forth across the open ribbon area 2 to 3 inches (5.1 to 7.6cm) from the surface.

NOTE: You may find it easier if you hold the stencil down with your fingers as you work each area.

4 With Dark Victorian Rose in the airbrush, repaint the deepest shading areas on the ribbon. Allow the color to fade into the Hibiscus you already painted. This will give a stronger look to the curve of the ribbon.

5 Airbrush the flowers in a circular motion with Light Blue Violet. Aim the color toward the outer part of the petals, letting the overspray fade toward the center of the flower.

6 Airbrush the leaves lightly with Baltic Green and remove the stencil. Allow the painted area to dry.

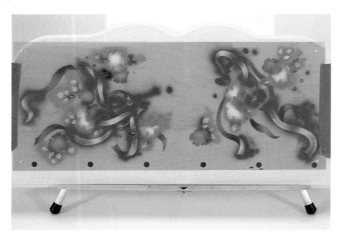

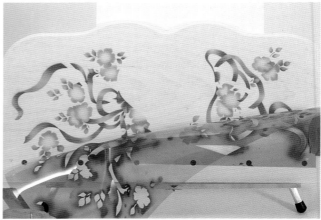

7 Carefully position stencil layer no. 2 to match the register marks, and tape it
in place. Repeat the process you used on the first layer, shading the ribbons
with Hibiscus first, deepening the shading with Dark Victorian Rose, and painting
the blossoms with Light Blue Violet. Then use Hooker's Permanent Green to shade
the base part of the leaves. Paint the small veins with this green also. When the
painted area is completely dry, remove the stencil.

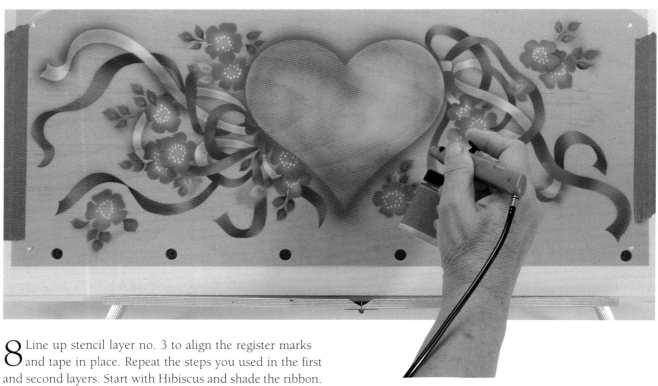

8 Line up stencil layer no. 3 to align the register marks
and tape in place. Repeat the steps you used in the first
and second layers. Start with Hibiscus and shade the ribbon.
Airbrush the heart lightly around the edges, and make a
circle on the highlight area to create a pattern for the darker
colors. This highlight is on the upper right-hand area in the
curve.

9 Still using Hibiscus, darken the heart color around the left side leaving a small edge. Then switch to Dark Victorian Rose and fill in around the circle highlight area. Use a continuous outline motion, allowing the color to fade into the highlight. And once you've filled in the heart, don't forget to deepen the ribbon shading as you did with the first and second layers.

10 Accent the outer edge of the heart on the left side (where you have the Hibiscus color showing) with a light line of Raw Sienna. Circle the highlight also, to round the heart and lift it out from the ribbons. Use this color lightly as an accent to create the illusion of three dimensions.

11 Airbrush the center dots of the flowers with Raw Sienna. Accent the tips of some of the lighter leaves with this color, and add a little to the leaf veins. Then remove the stencil.

12 Once the stencil layers are completed, add the pegs. Use waterbased varnish for the finish coat. To use the waterbased varnish in the airbrush, dilute it slightly to the consistency of 2% milk and apply three or four lightly misted layers to get good and even coverage.

Rose on Lace Doily

This project involves taking a pattern from a tole painting book and converting it to an airbrush design. The process requires many steps, but it is well worth the time and effort. You'll learn soft shading and glazing techniques and how to mix colors on the surface you're airbrushing.

I found the heart-shaped box in a tole painting shop. You could use a round surface with a round or heart-shaped doily, or a square box with a square doily (found in the cake decorating department of craft stores).

SUPPLIES

- Fine-point felt-tip pen
- Cutting surface and craft/hobby knife with no. 11 blade
- Sheets of matte-finish frisket film
- Repositionable spray adhesive (3M Spray Mount)
- Heart box or plaque (or the surface you've chosen)
- Sponge brush, soft cloth and Liquitex wood stain in Whitewash
- Paper lace heart doily
- Jo Sonja's acrylic paints: French Blue, Turner's Yellow, Chrome Oxide Green, Burgundy and Rose Pink

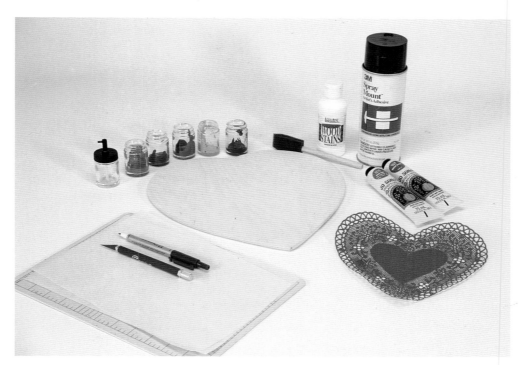

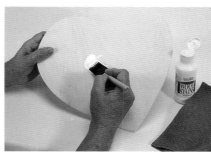

1 With a sponge or sponge brush apply Whitewash stain to the wood, moving in the direction of the grain.

2 Wipe off the excess stain with a soft cloth. Wipe in the direction of the wood grain for best results.

Pattern from *Hidden Treasures* published by Jean Zawicki (1988).
Use this drawing as your pattern. Paint the leaves in order from
A through G, and the rose petals in numerical order.

3 With a fine-point felt-tip pen, trace
the rose pattern onto the frisket.
Remove the frisket from the backing
and center the design on the painting
surface. Smooth the frisket from the
center out to eliminate air bubbles.
Trim the outer edge.

4 Cut out the leaves marked A, B, C,
D and E on the pattern. Remove
the frisket leaves and place them on the
backing you removed or on the outer
edge of the frisket to reserve them for
use in remasking after the leaves are
painted.

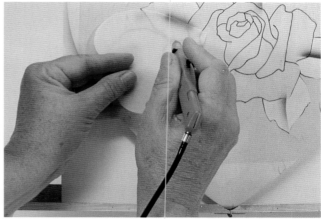

5 Place the long curve of the heart template on the center of each leaf. Using French Blue and holding the airbrush about 2 to 3 inches (5.1 to 7.6cm) above the surface, airbrush the center curved vein in each leaf from the base of the leaf outward. Try not to make the vein too dark toward the tip of the leaves. Repeat these last two steps with leaves marked F and G.

6 Place the tip of the heart template on the center vein near the base of each leaf. Working toward the tip, airbrush the secondary veins using the tip of the heart. The overspray will give the outer line of these veins the light look you want. Space the secondary veins evenly, about ¼ inch (0.6cm) apart.

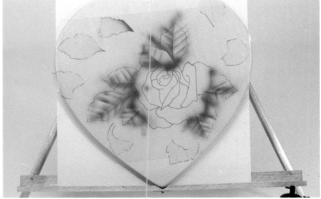

7 Add Turner's Yellow to the sides and tips of the leaves to create highlight. Pay attention to leaves that overlap another leaf as G over A.

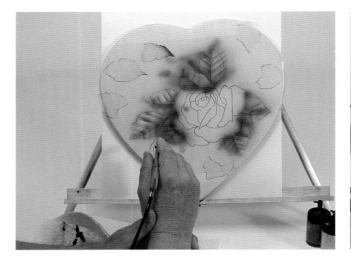 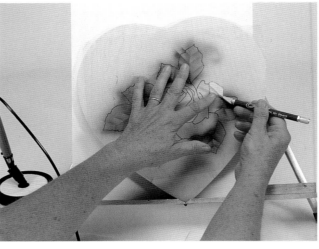

8 Using Chrome Oxide Green and holding the airbrush 4 inches (10.2cm) from the surface, create a soft flow of light color over the leaves. Glaze the leaves by airbrushing back and forth lightly and evenly over the open area. Allow the leaves to dry. Then carefully replace the frisket cutouts of the leaves in their original position and firmly press the edges.

9 Cut out and remove petals 1 and 2 and reserve the frisket pieces in case they are needed for solving problems later.

10 Adjust your airbrush for a light, small spray. Holding it 2 to 3 inches (5.1 to 7.6cm) above the surface, airbrush in the deep shaded areas with Burgundy. The shading should fade into the open area of the outer petal to form soft curves. Shade gradually into the open area, keeping the outer areas free of color.

11 Cut out petals 3 and 4 and reserve the frisket pieces. Airbrush the shaded areas in each petal in the same way you did petals 1 and 2. Refer to the shading pattern on this page for help.

12 Next, cut and shade petals 5, 6 and 12.

Refer to this diagram for basic shading patterns.

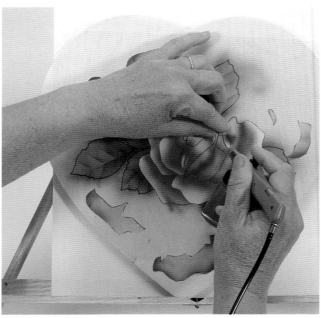

13 The areas marked 7 are line cuts that stop in the middle of a petal area. Cut to the end of this line, then turn back the frisket to the end of the cut, and airbrush a shadow in the area open under the cut. Allow the color to dry and replace the frisket.

14 Remove petal 8 (with the cut shaded) and airbrush a soft line down the center of the petal. This gives the look of a gentle fold. Allow it to dry and replace the frisket.

15 Remove petal 9 and shade the lower area.

16 Refer to the shading diagram. Note the Y-shaped shaded area on petal 10. Remove the frisket from petal 10 and shade.

17 Remove the frisket from petal 11. Shade down the center of the petal to give it a fold.

18 Shade the center petals in numerical order from 13 through 16. Don't hurry! Take time to look at each petal and place your shading carefully. Keep checking the shading diagram if you need help.

19 Here's my shaded rose.

20 With Rose Pink in the airbrush evenly glaze the entire rose with a light touch of color. If the color becomes too strong you will lose some of the shading. After you allow the color to dry, remove the frisket covering the leaves and add just a light touch of Rose Pink to the dark part of the leaves.

21 When the glazing is finished remove all the remaining frisket. Let the painted area dry thoroughly before going on to the next step.

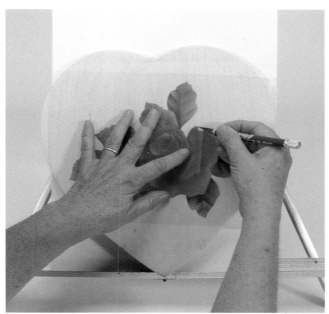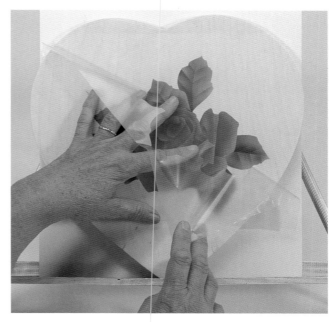

22 Re-cover the whole surface with a new sheet of frisket. Cut around the entire outer edge of the design and remove the background section of the frisket. This leaves the painted design masked.

23 Coat the paper lace doily on the right (or smoothest) side with a light film of repositionable adhesive. Allow the adhesive to set for a few minutes; then center the doily over the painted design. Adhere the doily firmly by pressing as evenly as possible from the center to the outer edge.

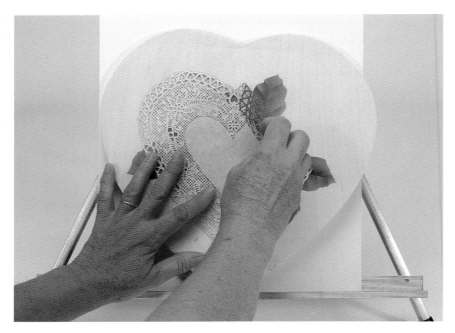

24 Airbrush with French Blue, starting with the inner solid part of the doily and moving outward until there is an area of strong color just outside the doily. Carefully remove the doily.

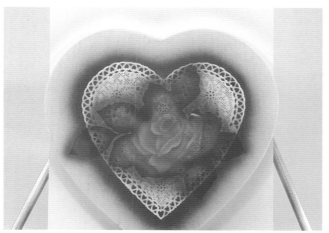

25 Without removing the frisket from the design area, add a bit of shading around the edge of the design. Use a light touch, building the color gradually. Remove the frisket.

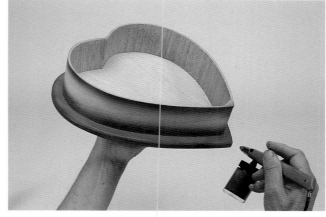

26 Holding the painted surface in your hand, airbrush the edges. Hold the airbrush 4 to 5 inches (10.2 to 12.7cm) from the surface, aiming toward the edge of the design. This will antique a soft French Blue around the outer area of the box top.

27 Antique the edges of the bottom of the box to match the top.

28 Here is the finished box, ready for a varnish finish. You can varnish with your airbrush if you use water-based varnish thinned to the consistency of 2% milk and spray on three or four light layers. When the surface is cure-dried in about two to three weeks, you can use a paste furniture wax, buffed for a soft look.

Old-Fashioned Girl

This is a lesson in "stencil reduction," wherein the stencil is cut away as the painting develops. This is a long lesson, so I suggest you read through it first and then follow the directions step by step. The design is rewarding and impressive as a finished piece. It could be done on a large oval board, even a large trunk.

SUPPLIES

- 11″ × 17″ (27.9cm × 43.2cm) sheet of frisket film
- Tavern or suitable size board stained with Liquitex Almond Wood Stain
- Liquitex Concentrated Artist Colors: Burnt Umber and Burnt Sienna, mixed half and half with water added (one part paint to one part water)
- 1 siphon cap and 1-ounce (28.4ml) bottle to fit airbrush
- Sponge brush and soft cloth for staining the wood
- Heart-shaped paper or vellum template
- Felt-tip pen
- Craft knife with no. 11 blade

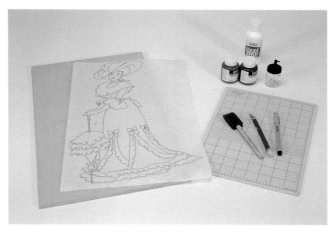

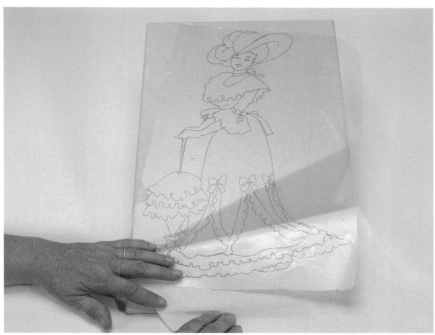

1 Trace the solid-line pattern shown on page 65 onto the frisket (the dotted lines are for reference only). Start removing the frisket backing. Center the pattern and pull the backing away while adhering the sticky side to the board. Smooth the frisket pattern from top to bottom to work out the air bubbles.

2 Cut along the solid line all around the figure and in the areas marked with an "X" on the pattern.

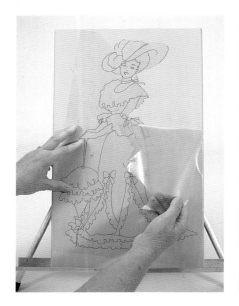  

3 Remove the background frisket carefully, pulling in a downward rolling motion. Areas with the "X" are removed next to allow the pattern to stand alone on the board.

 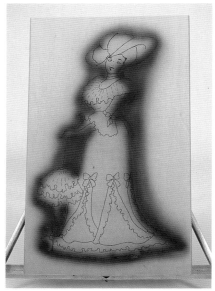 

4 With the Burnt Sienna/Burnt Umber color mix, begin airbrushing in the background. Your airbrush should be about 3 inches (7.6cm) from the surface to get a soft-edged spray of color. If you are getting a definite line in the spray pattern, back your hand away and allow more color to fade from the edges of the design. Work the color up slowly by using a continuous motion around the image and using layers of color to achieve the color density shown in the background. Straddle the edge of the design allowing some color to fall on the frisket. This will assure a clean inner edge all around the image.

5 To begin work on the figure, cut the bottom layer of the skirt ruffle frisket and remove it, leaving the area open for painting.

 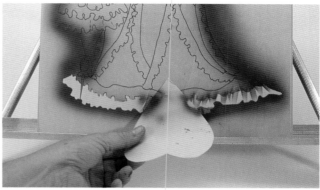

6 Place the pointed tip of the heart-shaped paper template at the top edge of the ruffle. Set a light spray pattern on the airbrush (if you are using an Aztek, rotate the silver wheel at the back to the left). At a distance of 1½ to 2 inches (3.8 to 5.1cm) from the surface, spray the small lines that fan from top to bottom on the ruffles to create fullness.

7 Go along in one direction from one end of the ruffle to the other, then switch to the other side of the template and reverse direction. This makes little triangle shapes in the ruffle so it looks as if it is fanning out.

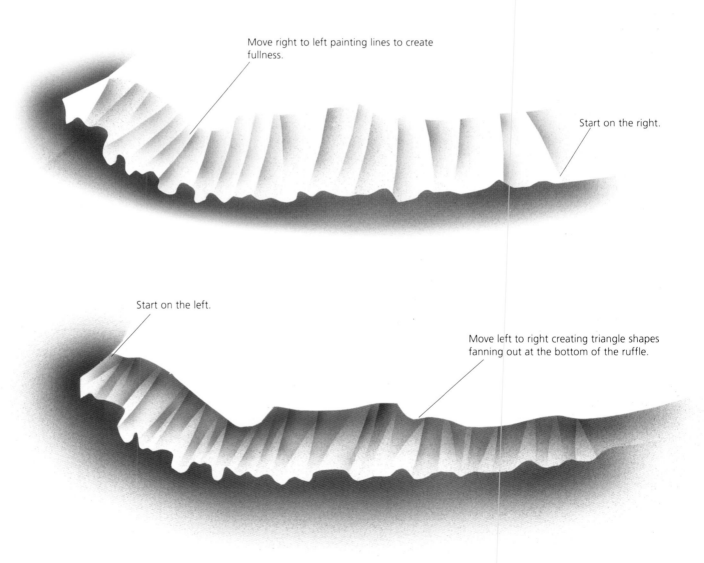

Move right to left painting lines to create fullness.

Start on the right.

Start on the left.

Move left to right creating triangle shapes fanning out at the bottom of the ruffle.

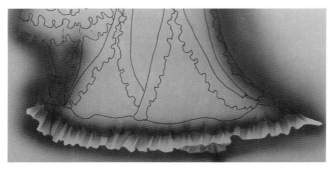

8 Next add a light shading along the top edge of the ruffle to give depth.

9 Cut away the next row of ruffle frisket and repeat steps 6 and 7, being careful not to allow the spray to continue into the ruffle you have just finished at the bottom.

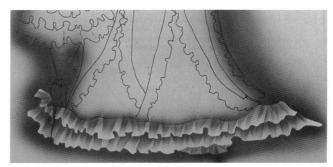

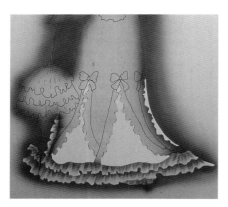
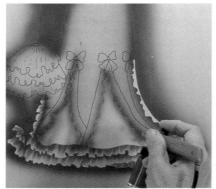
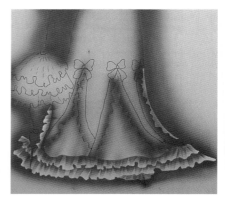

10 Cut away the frisket in the areas under the skirt ruffles and shade them using an up-and-down motion. The areas where the skirt has an upward curve at the bottom are left light for a highlight and the soft folds where the skirt dips toward the bottom are shaded with a soft spray pattern.

Next airbrush the side ruffles on the skirt. Deepen the shade area under the side ruffles before cutting out the ruffles.

11 Cut away the ruffle frisket under the skirt panel on the left side. Airbrush the ruffles at a slight angle to give the look of hanging toward the bottom of the skirt.

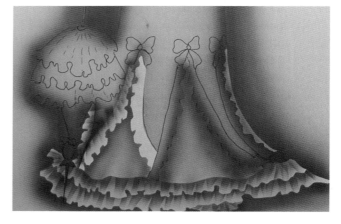

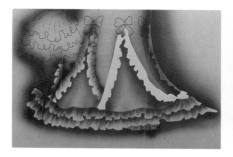  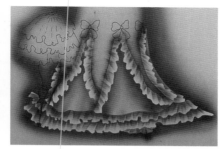

12 Cut away the ruffle frisket in sequence from left to right and airbrush, using the heart-shaped template on page 66 and the ruffle technique shown on page 57. Finish all the ruffles on the skirt area.

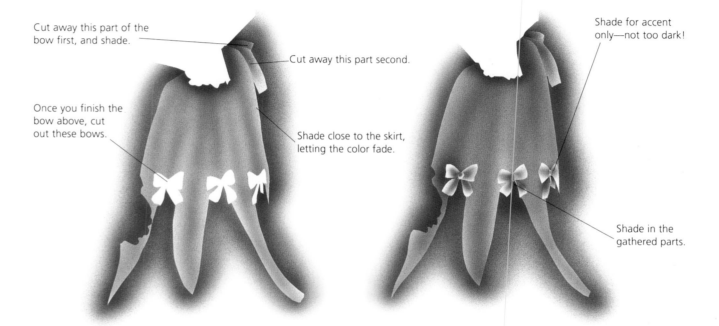

Cut away this part of the bow first, and shade.

Cut away this part second.

Once you finish the bow above, cut out these bows.

Shade close to the skirt, letting the color fade.

Shade for accent only—not too dark!

Shade in the gathered parts.

13 Remove the skirt area of the frisket, cutting around the parasol and bows. Airbrush the shadow behind the sleeve lace and along the arm area. This shadow is fairly dark and fades into the skirt shading. The skirt shading is done with an up-and-down motion to create folds.

The bows are done with just a touch of shading in the gathered parts near the center. Accent the deeper areas at the center of the loops and ties.

Shade gathered areas of ties first.

Shade loops, masking center knot if necessary.

Put a dot of shading in the center knot.

Leave edges for highlight.

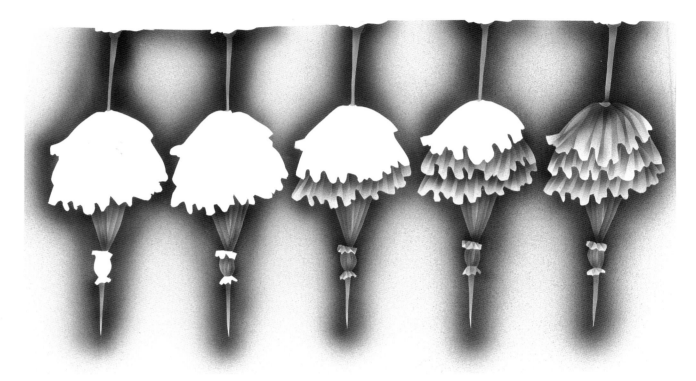

14 The handle of the parasol is done first. Then the ruffles are done step by step in the same manner as the ruffles at the bottom of the skirt, from lowest to highest. Here and there where the ruffles are longer, use the slight curve on the edge of the heart template.

15 Cut and remove the frisket from the smooth neckline area just above the large ruffle, the back arm holding the parasol and the lower bodice area.

16 Shade these areas lightly (follow the dotted line on the pattern) with a soft spray pattern from about 2 inches (5.1cm) away to give a soft line to the bosom area.

17 Remove frisket from the three small areas shown. Shade the long sleeve area and the forward glove area with slight finger definition. The back lace sleeve is detailed with ruffles.

18 The ruffles on the lace collar and the forward sleeve are shaded next. Use a long slight curve on the heart template. The outer edges of the lace on the collar should be left very light to enhance the fullness of the ruffle and to give the body dimension.

19 Expose the back area under the hat and the neck above the ribbon. Airbrush the hat area dark, and the neck area a medium value just under the chin.

21 Cut away the left-side ear and hat brim and lightly shade.

22 Remove the frisket from the hair section and the lower feather on the hat. Fill in these areas with a soft upward motion of the airbrush. NOTE: Turn on the airbrush just on the frisket, then as you lift your arm in an upward motion, slowly turn off the airbrush by allowing the trigger to move forward. This will give you the soft lines for texturing the hair and the feathers in the hat.

20 The back of the hair next to the hat is cut to the curve and the curve area is cut to the line end. Pull back the cut area between the hair and the hat and shade along the open curve area. When that's dry, replace the turned-back area of the frisket.

23 Remove the frisket from the center feather and airbrush in an upward motion. Then peel frisket from the left ear and shade it.

24 Remove the last piece of frisket from the feather area and shade the forward feather in an upward motion.

25 Cut and remove the frisket on the facial features, then airbrush them using a few light coats to achieve the dark lines.

NOTE: Because these are very small areas, too much paint at one time could smear under the edges or load up on the frisket and cause blobs. A few coats, lightly done, are best.

26 Remove the frisket from the face. With a light touch and a light spray pattern, shade the face around the outside hairline. This will give the face a rounded look. Shade lightly across the eyes from hairline to hairline, and underneath the hat brim.

27 Remove frisket from the large hat brim and lightly shade down the center of the open area to give the brim the look of a softly curved fold.

28 Antique the finished board with a bit of color along the edges for a balanced look. If you are not adding the "Lilac Tea Room" signs to the finished board, then let it dry thoroughly for two to three weeks. Varnish with several light coats. Any cuts in the wood will be "healed" with the varnish.

Pattern by Eleanor Zimmerman from her book *Great Grandma's Garb* published by Zim's, Inc. of Salt Lake City, Utah (1990).

Use the dotted lines as guides for shading.

Cut out the areas marked with an X when you remove the background.

Small cluster of blossoms here.

Dotted lines show overall shape of lilacs.

Small clusters of blossoms

Large cone-shaped clusters of blossoms

Shading template

Small stencil for lilac blossoms

"Lilac Tea Room" Sign Boards

If you would like to add the sign boards to the "Old-Fashioned Girl" project, trace the patterns at left onto tracing paper or vellum. Transfer the patterns to frisket with a permanent felt-tip pen. Peel off the backing and apply the frisket sticky side down to the stained wood. Trace the heart template onto vellum and cut it out.

SUPPLIES

- 2 boards made with grooves to slide over the top and bottom of the Old-Fashioned Girl board
- 2 sheets frisket, matte finish
- Felt-tip pen
- Liquitex Concentrated Artist Colors: Baltic Green, Wisteria, French Gray-Blue, Light Blue Violet and the Burnt Umber/Burnt Sienna color mix

1 Cut out the leaves and save them on the pattern for future masking.

2 With Baltic Green, airbrush the leaves.

3 With the Burnt Umber/Burnt Sienna mix, shade the leaves at the base lightly and vein the center of the leaves with a heart template. Allow to dry and then replace the frisket shapes over the leaves.

4 Cut and remove the lettering frisket. Airbrush with two or more light coats of Wisteria to get strong coverage. (The Wisteria color is semitransparent and the coverage will be smoother if you apply several light coats, allowing each to dry slightly before adding the next.)

5 Remove all the frisket except over the leaves.

6 To make the cone-shaped lilac blossoms, spray dots of the Wisteria color by turning the airbrush on and off from 1 to 2 inches (2.5 to 5.1cm) away from the surface. Refer to the dotted areas on the pattern. Make the color stronger by spraying more often at the bottom of the cone shapes and in the center of the shape.

7 Cut out the small blossom stencil on page 66. Airbrush petal definition by placing the stencil near the edges of the dots and airbrush through it using Wisteria.

8 Scatter small blossoms randomly in the open areas. Remove the frisket covering the leaves.

9 Repeat steps 7 and 8 with French Gray-Blue color.

10 Using the small blossom stencil, spray Light Blue Violet randomly over the blossom areas to give the flowers dimension. This is done sparingly to enhance the colors.

11 Let dry. The signs are now ready for antiquing.

12 With the Burnt Umber/Burnt Sienna mix, lightly airbrush the edges of the boards to achieve a dusting of color around the flat surface of the board. Darken if necessary to match the "Old-Fashioned Girl" board.

Slide the tea room signs onto the main board before varnishing. Use several coats of waterbased varnish thinned to the consistency of 2% milk. Let it dry thoroughly. If you wish, wax the boards with furniture paste wax and buff for a soft finish look.

Holiday Ornament

Begin this project with a flat circle and transform it into a three-dimensional ball. This is a basic exercise in technique, and you'll find all sorts of ways to use it. You'll do the shading first, the images second and the background last. Then add starbursts for interest—and to cover goofs—after everything else is finished.

While the design is used here on a photo album, it would also be good on a wooden box for storing ornaments, a notebook, or reduced and airbrushed on an address book for your holiday card list. The surface should be white or off-white.

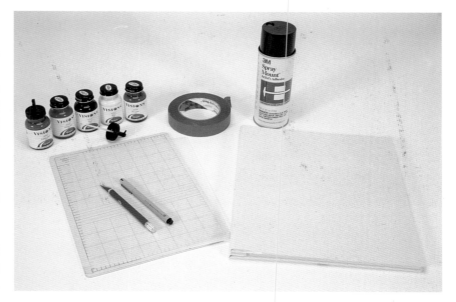

SUPPLIES
- 1 sheet stencil film
- Cutting mat, stencil/hobby knife with no. 11 blade
- Scotch 3M Long-Mask Masking Tape
- Repositionable spray adhesive (3M Spray Mount)
- Fine-line permanent felt-tip pen
- Canvas-covered photo album (the one shown is by Dalee Book Co.)
- Visions Opaque paints: Holiday Red, Holiday Green, Black, White and Pine Green
- Siphon cap bottle lids with long dip tubes (for 2-ounce [56.8ml] bottles of Visions)

1 Enlarge the design on page 72 and trace it on the stencil film with a permanent felt-tip marker. Using the knife, cut on all the lines. Spray all the pieces with repositionable adhesive and place them on the album cover in their original position.

NOTE: Lightly spray the repositional adhesive from 8 to 12 inches (20.3 to 30.5cm) above the stencil film. Allow it to set for a few minutes before adhering the pieces to the painting surface.

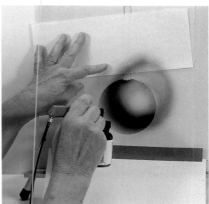

2 Remove the stencil film from the ball. Shade the ball with Black using a circular motion 2 to 3 inches (5.1 to 7.6cm) from the surface. Refer to the shading diagram. Notice how the shading is applied in a circle the size of the opening but painted off center. The color is graduated within the color band, the heaviest being in the center of the band.

NOTE: As a shortcut, you may choose to remove the stencil film from the ribbon at the same time you remove the stencil film from the ball. If you do, you'll need to use a piece of paper to mask the ribbon while you shade the ball, as shown.

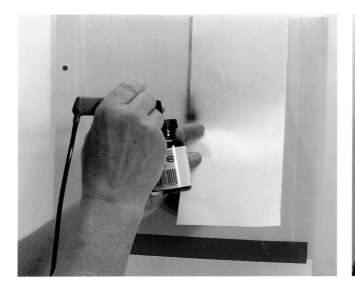 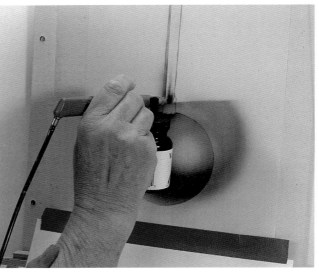

3 If you haven't already done so, remove the ribbon part of the stencil film. Shade along the length of the ribbon to show the fold. You can use the same paper you used in the previous step as a sharp edge. Position the paper slightly to the right of the left side of the ribbon.

4 Airbrush small streaks of Black for folds at the base of the ribbon where it goes through the loop.

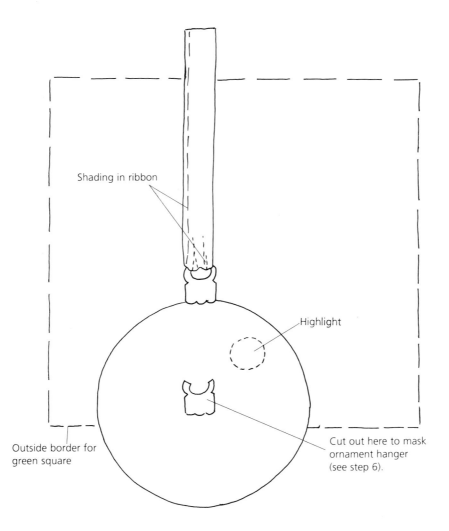

Shading in ribbon

Highlight

Outside border for
green square

Cut out here to mask
ornament hanger
(see step 6).

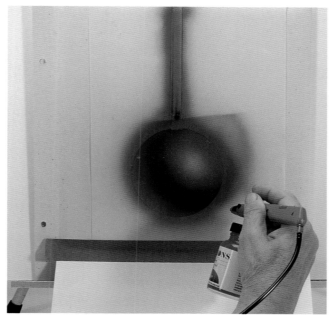
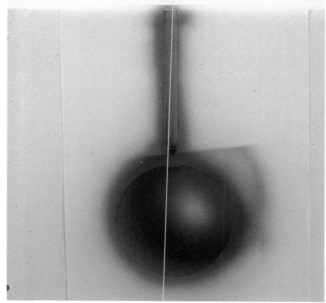

5 Airbrush the ribbon and ball with Holiday Red. Use a circular motion on the ball similar to the motion used in the shading, leaving the highlight white at the right of the center.

6 Remove the stencil film to expose the ornament hanger. Also remove the ornament hanger piece from the center of the ball. Position the stencil film as a mask.

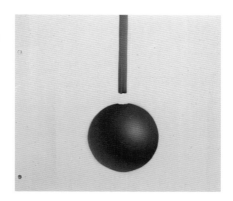

Use this shading diagram as a reference for shading the ball.

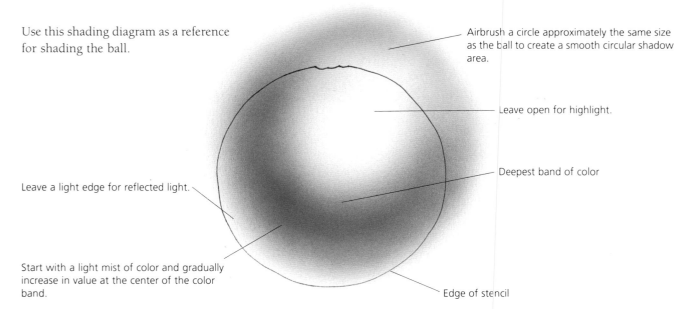

Airbrush a circle approximately the same size as the ball to create a smooth circular shadow area.

Leave open for highlight.

Deepest band of color

Leave a light edge for reflected light.

Start with a light mist of color and gradually increase in value at the center of the color band.

Edge of stencil

7 Mix Black and White to create a soft gray. Paint the ornament hanger with the light gray and allow it to dry.

8 Replace the stencil parts on the ribbon, ball and ornament hanger, pushing them down to hold them in place. Cover with tape the opening on the ball where you cut out the ornament hanger. Tape strips of paper all around the design area to form a background square. They block off areas you want to keep clear of color. The ornament should drop below the bottom line of the taped-off square.

9 With Holiday Green in the airbrush, paint color in the background. Allow it to be a bit blotchy and do not worry about getting the color smooth. The look you are going for is the suggestion of holiday greenery all around.

10 Repeat airbrushing the background with Pine Green. Concentrate heavier color around the ball and in the lower right corner.

11 Now let's add some sparkling starbursts. First, brace your arm to steady it. One inch (2.5cm) from the surface (closer if you need to) airbrush dots using White. Scatter the dots randomly and vary the size.

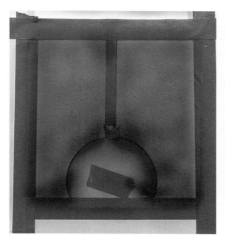
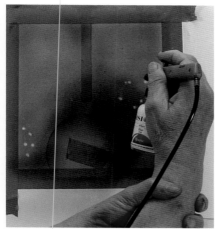

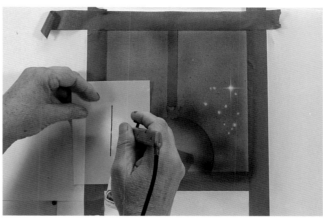
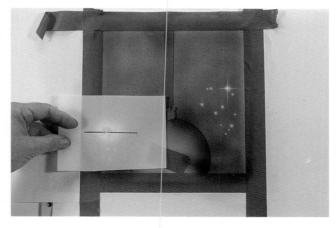

12 Hold the starburst slot stencil vertically and center it over a dot. Airbrush White from 2 to 2½ inches (5.1 to 6.4cm) from the surface, holding the airbrush absolutely still. Spray at the center of the slot *without* moving. You will allow the overspray to graduate the color above and below the dot.

13 Move the slot stencil to a horizontal position over the same dot. Again without moving, airbrush over the center of the slot. Remove the stencil and very slowly airbrush a soft area at the center where the two rays cross. Repeat these two steps for each of the white dots to create the starbursts. (For more on starbursts, see pages 22-25.)

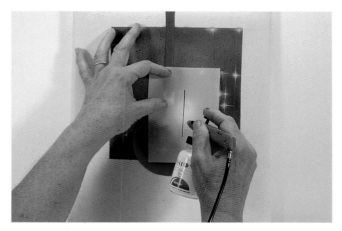
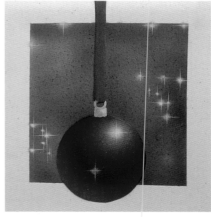

14 Remove the stencil parts and the taped paper masks from the painted area. Airbrush a starburst at the center of the highlight on the ball and a small one in the dark lower area of color on the ornament.

15 Use starbursts to disguise areas where the tape was loose and allowed color to leak. They'll cover the goofs and add depth.

Faux Finishes: Wood Grain Box

Wood graining is a great way to decorate a papier-mâché box because the base color is already there. For a country-look gift box you can add a raffia bow and some wild flowers on top. For a less casual look, wallpaper the inside of the box. This technique can also be used on a ceramic piece to give the look of wood carving. However, any piece other than a natural kraft papier-mâché finish should be basecoated a soft tan color. Use a Burnt Umber with a wide spray pattern and allow a bit of uneven color to occur as you airbrush. This will give texture to the wood look.

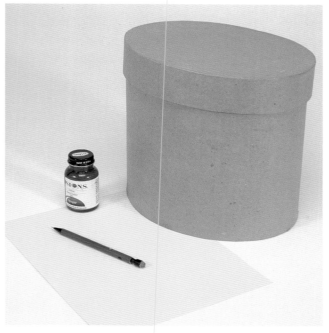

SUPPLIES

- Papier-mâché box (or suitable piece)
- Opaque colors, any brand prepared for airbrush: Burnt Umber, Burnt Sienna, Black
- Soft lead pencil
- Ruler or straightedge

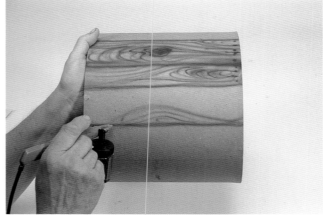

1 Decide whether you'd like a casual look with boards of varying widths, or a more formal, less country look with boards of uniform size. Using a ruler or straightedge, draw pencil lines all around the box. These pencil lines should be up and down along the sides of the box, and across on the top. The edge of the top is treated as small boards curved around the circumference of the box.

2 Using Burnt Umber in your airbrush, paint along the board lines you drew. This should be fairly dark and well defined to create separations between the boards. Straight lines are newer boards; the wobbly ones are old barn wood, so don't worry if your lines aren't perfect. Make cracks at the board ends and add nail holes. Just a dot of color creates a nail hole.

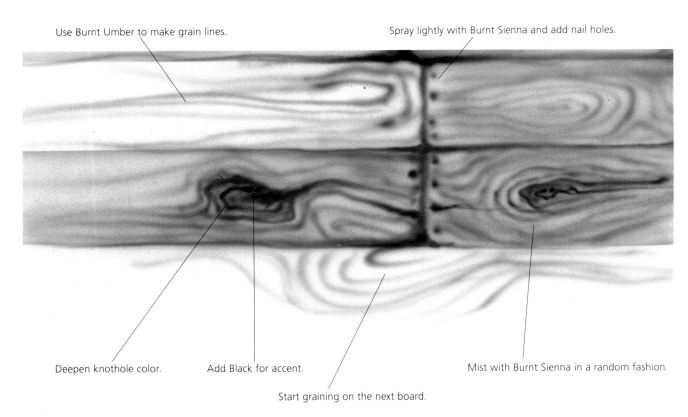

Use Burnt Umber to make grain lines.

Spray lightly with Burnt Sienna and add nail holes.

Deepen knothole color.

Add Black for accent.

Mist with Burnt Sienna in a random fashion.

Start graining on the next board.

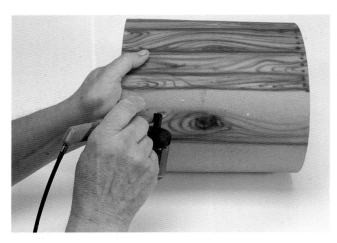

3 Add grain lines to the boards in random patterns. I usually start with a small curve in the open areas (not always centered), and then I repeat the curve moving out and allowing the airbrush line to get wider and fuzzy. I make several lines as I move outward. I carry the last repeat into a reverse curve as it moves around the circle and down into the next grain line.

4 Add grain patterns to all your "boards." Relax and enjoy using your airbrush. There are no rules here. The more random the boards are in relation to each other the more realistic it will look. Each wood has its own grain pattern, so whatever you create will be fine.

5 Once you finish the sides of the box, add grain lines to the boards on the lid. Then switch colors and use Black to accent the wood grain. Add depth and detail to knothole areas and add definition between boards. Here and there add crispness to your grain patterns, but don't go overboard.

6 When you have completely "boarded" your box, lightly shade around the edges with Burnt Umber to soften and age the wood.

7 With Burnt Sienna in the airbrush, and from a distance of 3 or 4 inches (7.6 or 10.2cm), spray color in a loose pattern to give more color to the wood. This will give dimension to the project. Use a satin- or matte-finish varnish when the color is completely dry. Several coats will give the best effect. If you wish, line the box with wallpaper to create a functional keepsake.

Faux Finishes: Granite Box

This easy and fun faux finish is great for creating gifts and can even be used to restore old table tops. The box in this lesson is about the size of the old cigar box I kept my crayons stashed in during grade school. Instead of a box, you could use a board if it doesn't have fancy routed edges. You might also use the design on a sweatshirt if you paint with airbrush-formulated fabric dye.

The type of airbrush you use is important for this project. I used an Aztek 3000S with a splatter nozzle. You could use the Visions Air-Painter or a single-action external-mix airbrush for this job, but you'll have to experiment with it to get it to spatter.

SUPPLIES

- **Creative box from Walnut Hollow (#1253), or any paintable wood or papier-mâché box**
- **1 sheet stencil film**
- **Cutting knife with no. 11 blade and mat**
- **Sanding pad for prepping the box**
- **Size no. 1 liner brush**
- **Liquitex Concentrated Artist Colors: Neutral Gray Value 5, Titanium White (or Visions Opaque Slate Gray and White), Chromium Oxide Green, Vivid Red Orange (in a tube), Maroon, Black**
- **Scotch 3M Long-Mask Masking Tape**
- **Pencil**

1 Sand the box to smooth rough edges and get loose wood particles out of the way. With the gray color, basecoat the box and inner lid edges that will be seen. When the basecoat is dry, lightly sand the raised grain on the wood, but do not remove the paint. Wipe with a slightly damp cloth or a tack cloth. Sand again to remove the rough spots the first coat raised in the wood grain and apply a second coat of gray.

Using the pink spatter nozzle on the Aztek 3000S airbrush and Black paint in the large side cup, spatter the entire box.
NOTE: Practice first. Pull the trigger back to allow paint to enter the airbrush system and then depress the trigger for air. The lighter the pressure for air, the larger the spattering will be. This will take a little practice but is worth the effort.

2 If you accidentally get a large spatter, take the no. 1 liner brush and pull the paint from the center of the splat. Drag the tip of the brush lightly to create a crack in the stone. Allow the color to fade as you pull the stroke, and make it jagged. But to prevent accidents, watch the tip of your airbrush. If you notice a drop of color collecting on the tip, wipe it off. When you practice you will get a feel for the right amount of air and paint.

3 Clean the color cup and fill it with White. Spatter the complete box again—maybe a little finer this time—and allow it to dry. This will give you a chance to lighten areas left too dark from the Black spattering. Clean the airbrush again and replace the spatter nozzle with the gray all-purpose nozzle.

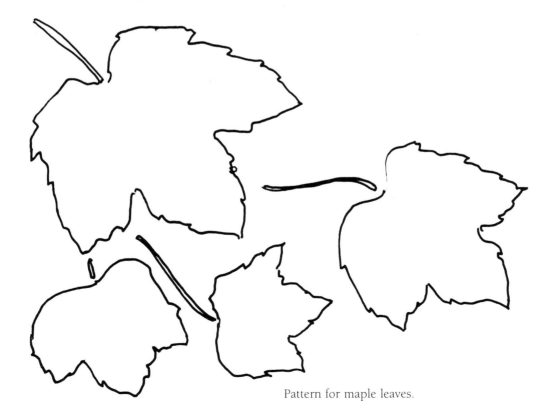

Pattern for maple leaves.

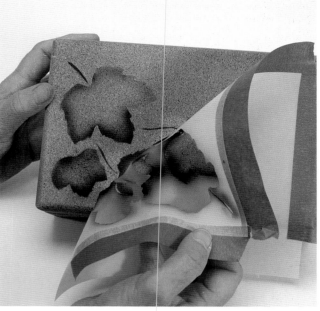

4 Trace the maple leaf design onto the stencil film. Cut out the maple leaves and stems. Tape the stencil to the box top, placing the design where you want the finished leaves. With the pencil, mark the right and upper sides of the leaves on the painting surface. Then move the stencil down ¼ inch (0.6cm) and to the left ¼ inch (0.6cm) and tape it firmly.

5 With Black in the airbrush paint the shading in, lightly at the top of the leaves, and stronger at the bottom and left side of each leaf and the stems. (For more on creating shadows, see the Ivy Key Holder project, pages 30-35.) Remove the stencil and allow the paint to dry.

6 Replace the stencil to the original position by lining the leaves up to the pencil marks you made, and tape it in place.

7 Airbrush the leaves with Chromium Oxide Green. Allow this color to be a bit random and blotchy. *Do not* try to cover all the Black paint that shows through.

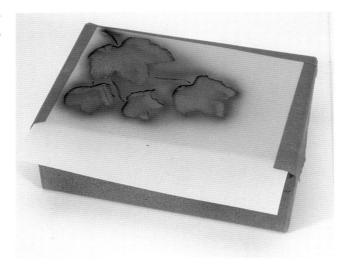

8 With Vivid Red Orange, and using a heart template, airbrush the veins in the leaves and light areas at the top and edges of the leaves. (See Veining Leaves, pages 16-17.)

9 Glaze evenly over the entire leaf areas and stems with Maroon. You should be 2 to 3 inches (5.1 to 7.6cm) from the surface with the airbrush on a fine, light spray pattern. This should look transparent and allow a bit of the green and orange to show through. This is a very strong and transparent color so be careful not to use too much. Build up the color with light coats.

10 If you want to age the granite, use White thinned with water and lightly airbrush the edges of the box (in a manner similar to antiquing) where rubbing or weathering would wear away the edge.

Faux-Marbled Cherub

This is a fun way to create accents and to renew old tabletops on small tables or nightstands. I used a plaster cherub from the craft store, but almost any wood item, or plaster or bisque ceramic will work. If you're used to using stencils and working with more precise designs, this technique may seem strange to you. It's random and free-flowing, and you may wonder if it will turn out right. Relax and have fun! And if the results do not please you the first time, take a fifteen-minute break. Come back and look again, and if necessary, spray the piece Black and start all over. I suspect you'll be so pleased that you'll want to try marbling again.

I suggest two different airbrushes for this project, but you can use only one. The Visions AirPainter applies a lot of color fast, and is great for the basecoat of Black and applying the Green and White. However, for the veining you'll need the Aztek 3000S. You can use the Aztek for the entire project if you wish.

SUPPLIES

- Plaster item (or bisque ceramic)
- Small sea sponge (can also be called a wool or silk sponge) with large uneven holes
- Visions AirPainter and canned air
- Visions Opaques: Black, Holiday Green, White
- Aztek 3000S airbrush for veining detail
- Waterbased varnish for finish

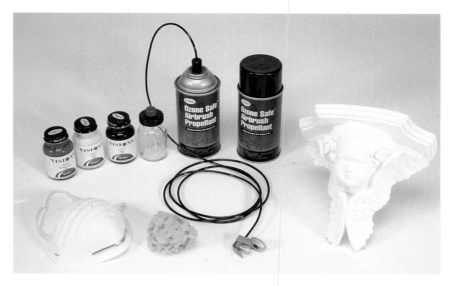

1 Sand the plaster piece if necessary to remove any rough spots. Then basecoat the entire piece with Black, taking care to turn it and check all the bumps and crevices to be sure they are covered.

2 Connect the AirPainter to the bottle of Holiday Green, and to the canned air or a compressor. With your painting hand use the AirPainter. Hold a slightly damp sea sponge in the other hand. Spray a small area with the Holiday Green, and while it is still wet, lightly stipple-pat it with the damp sponge. You will pick up color as you do this and it will rearrange itself when you use the sponge on the surface again. As it dries, the color will soften the Black and blend the Green. Repeat this in small areas and randomly cover the whole surface.

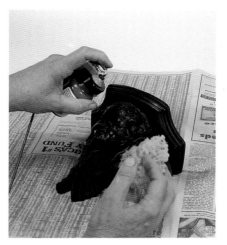

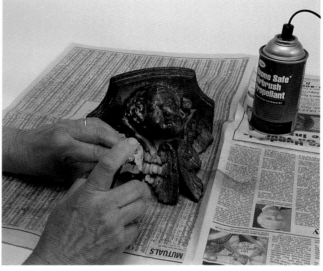

3 Rinse out the sponge and switch to White in your airbrush. Repeat the sponging technique from the previous step. Create a random pattern over the Black and Green. Keep the White lighter and spread out a bit more than you did with the Green. The three colors will blend slightly and take on a marbled look as the paint dries. When there are no wet shiny spots visible, it's safe to go on.

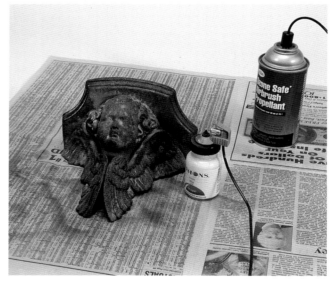

4 Using Black in the Aztek 3000S, set the spray pattern to a fine-line, dual-action mode and airbrush, almost touching the surface. Create random vein lines across the features. The veins are characteristic of the marble itself, so you shouldn't worry about following design contours. Think of lightning in the sky—this is the look you want.

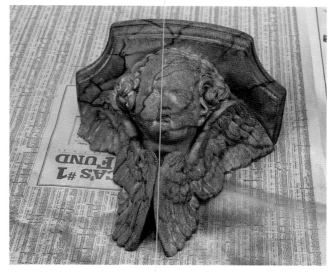

Green-and-Black Marbling

| Black basecoat | Holiday Green wet sponged as it is applied | White sponged over Green and Black | Veining airbrushed with White and Black |

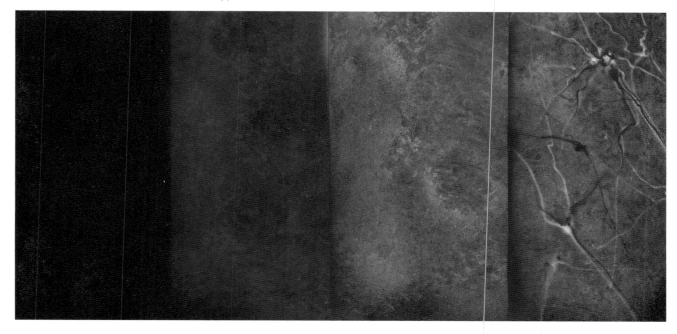

5 Repeat the veining technique using White. Echo the Black veining here and there by dragging a white vein alongside a black one. It really will look like lightning then!

NOTE: Remember to relax. This should be fun. If the results do not please you the first time, repeat from step 1 and redo the whole project before varnishing.

6 The finish is up to you. A matte varnish will give a soft-patina look to the marble as if it were aged. A high gloss will give it a just-polished look. Whatever finish you decide is best, use several light coats and work up the surface texture gradually.

Norwegian Rose Marble Use this as an alternative faux marbling color.

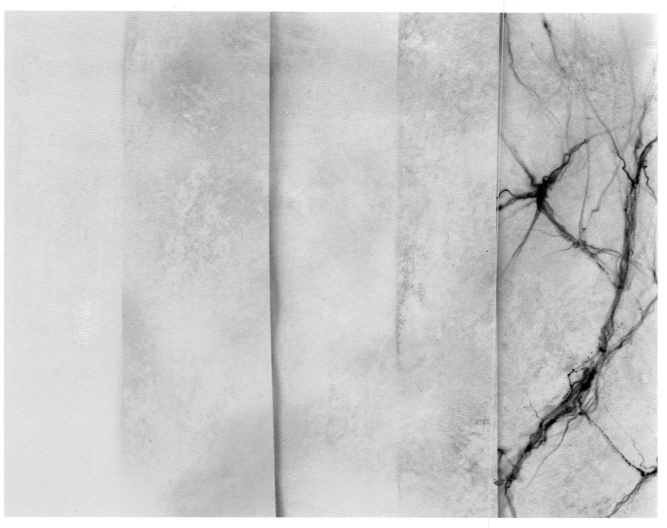

Mix White and Burnt Sienna or Raw Sienna to create an off-white base color.

Use a rose color (this is Visions Apricot) and wet sponge over the basecoat.

Sponge White sparsely over the rose color.

Wet sponge Burnt Sienna sparingly, or randomly airbrush from a distance of 3 to 6 inches (7.6 to 15.2cm).

Widely space veins with Burnt Sienna and detail with a touch of Black.

Antique Spanish Tiles

I thought it would be fun to make a table with a faux tile top as an accent piece. This technique could also be used on the top of a box, or reduced on a small sewing kit. The pattern is a simple single-layer stencil. Nothing has to be blocked out as you use it because the areas are separate and open.

The table I used is made by Whittier and is available at craft and unfinished furniture stores all over the country. If you are going to refurbish an old table you will have to sand the top to get a good tooth. This is so the crackle medium will adhere well. Use a dark brown basecoat or stain. And because some of the supplies you need are not pictured, pay particular attention to the list of supplies below.

SUPPLIES

- **W.N. Wonder & Co., Inc. 1881 Crackle Medium in Brown. (If you use another brand of crackle medium, use clear and follow their directions to achieve the brown color base for the crackle surface.)**
- **Liquitex Concentrated Artist Colors: Titanium White, Raw Sienna, Burnt Umber; Visions Eggshell (optional)**
- **Paint brushes: no. 4 flat hand brush, no. 0 or no. 1 liner**
- **ComArt Medea transparent airbrush colors: Cadmium Yellow, Emerald Green, Ultramarine Blue, Red, Black and Sienna Brown. (All these colors are available in a primary color kit from Medea.)**
- **1 sheet of stencil film, cutting knife and mat**
- **Liquitex Wood Stain: English Oak**
- **Permanent fine-line felt-tip pen**
- **Sponges and sponge brush for staining, paper towels, soft cloth**

1 Apply wood stain freely with the sponge brush. Follow the grain of the wood as you apply the stain.

NOTE: Keep your bare hands off the stain until it is wiped. I wear rubber gloves or put a paper towel between my hand and the surface I am staining.

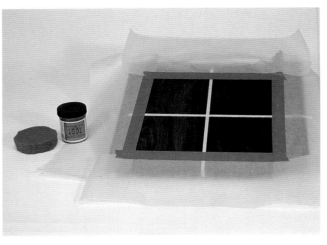

2 Wipe off the excess wood stain with a cloth or absorbent paper towels. Allow the wood to dry completely, preferably overnight.

3 Tape off on the inside area of the tiles with ¼-inch (0.6cm) masking tape. Be sure the edges of the tape are straight and secure. Each tile measures 5¼ inches (13.3cm) square. Measure; then mark the outside edges with a pencil. Using the masking tape and paper, tape off the outside edge of the tiles.

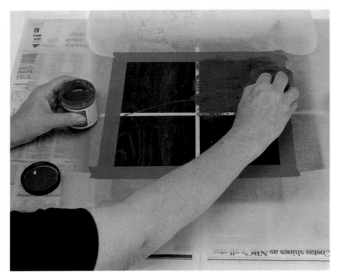

4 Apply the crackle medium with a sponge using a dabbing or stippling motion. The stippling motion for coverage is to create a slightly lumpy texture without any sponge strokes. Be sure the coverage is overall, fairly thick and free of bubbles. Before you go on, the surface must be dry to the touch. Speed up the process if you wish by using a hair dryer set to low or medium heat.

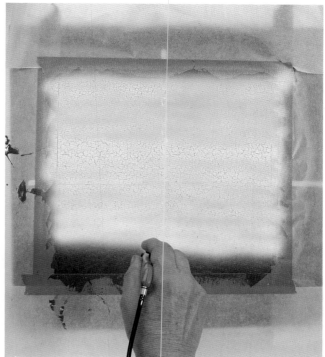

5 With Titanium White and Raw Sienna, mix an ivory or off-white color to basecoat the tile surface. Or if you prefer not to mix the colors, use the color called Eggshell by Visions. Open the airbrush to its fullest volume (setting the silver wheel at the back of the Aztek 3000S all the way to the right by pushing down and pulling back on the trigger as far as possible). This creates the heaviest paint load, essential for the crackle effect.

You need to pace yourself to allow a heavy paint volume on the first strip across because you can't go back. Work across the area from side to side, slightly overlapping the faint part of edges as you go. *Do not* go over the first layer of paint! If you do, the crackle will be covered and the cracking will not happen. As the paint and the crackle set up together, the cracking design begins to occur. By the time you are painting the last row of color, the cracking design will already be following you and extending below the center of the board.

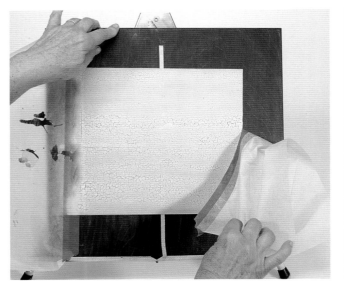 

6 Before the basecoat is thoroughly dry, begin to remove the outer tape and paper. Use a "rolling back" motion to get a clean line along the tape edges. Carefully remove the ¼-inch (0.6cm) tape between the tiles as well, using the roll-back motion. Allow this basecoat to dry.

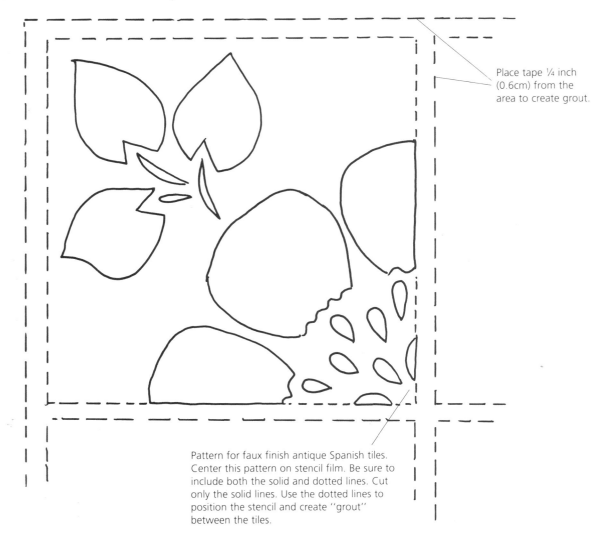

Place tape ¼ inch (0.6cm) from the area to create grout.

Pattern for faux finish antique Spanish tiles. Center this pattern on stencil film. Be sure to include both the solid and dotted lines. Cut only the solid lines. Use the dotted lines to position the stencil and create "grout" between the tiles.

7 Trace the stencil design onto the stencil film and cut out the design components. Position the stencil on one of the tiles with the seeds at the center of the 4-tile section. With masking tape attach the stencil to the surface where there is wood stain. Do not attach tape to the basecoat area.

8 Load your airbrush with the ComArt Medea Transparent Cadmium Yellow. (I've found that with these ComArt colors, a little goes a long way. I used a medium gravity cup for the Aztek 3000S with only a little paint. When I finished with each color, I wiped out the cup, poured in the next color and airbrushed on paper towels until the new color came out clean.) With the Yellow, airbrush the seeds and the center section of the large petals. Add a little to the center of the leaves also. Wipe out the cup for the next color. NOTE: The transparent colors are best used in several light coats. Build up the color slowly for the smoothest surface.

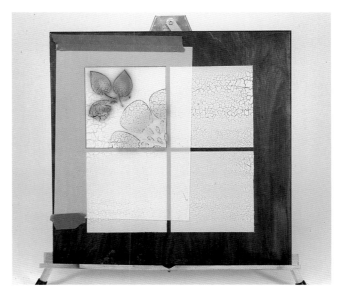

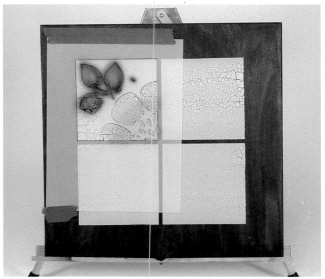

9 Using Transparent Emerald Green, airbrush the stems and lightly tint the leaves. Wipe out the cup and pour in the Transparent Ultramarine Blue.

10 With Transparent Ultramarine Blue add a touch of color around the outer edges of the leaves. Wipe out the cup and pour in Transparent Red.

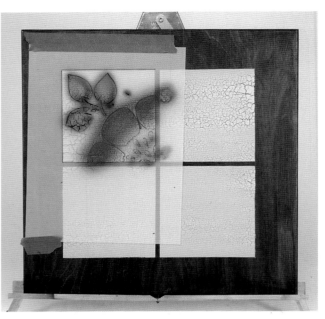

11 Use Transparent Red to airbrush the outer edge of the large flower petals. Allow the color to fade or blend into the yellow areas. Wipe out the cup again and switch to Transparent Sienna Brown.

12 With Transparent Sienna Brown shade the pointed tip of each yellow seed.

13 Carefully remove the stencil and allow the painted area to dry.

14 Position the stencil on the lower left of the surface. Repeat steps 8 through 12 to complete the second tile. Use the colors in the same order as before, and allow the crackle to show through. This gives the look of old tiles.

 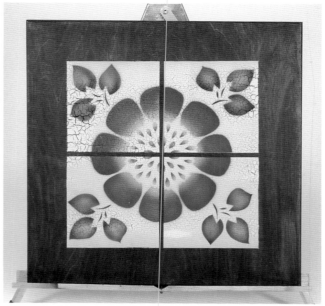

15 Repeat the steps you've done before to complete the other two tiles. Try to make each tile look like the first, but don't worry if there is some variation. Even authentic tiles have slight differences.

16 With a no. 1 liner brush, I used the Transparent Black airbrush paint to outline the color areas of the design. If you like how your tiles look without this detail, leave it out. The original tiles were done both ways.

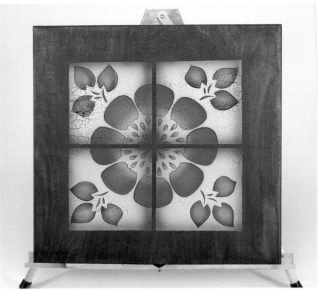

17 Allow the tiles to dry completely. Then use Burnt Umber in the airbrush to lightly outline all the way around each tile. Keep the spray fairly steady, and don't allow the amount of overspray you would if you were antiquing.

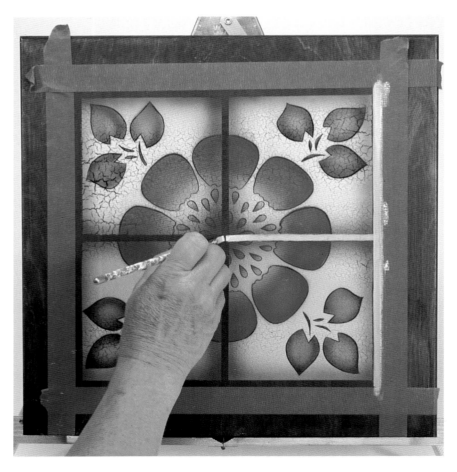

18 With masking tape, mask off ¼ inch (0.6cm) from the edge of the tiles all around the outside. With a hand brush (no. 2 or no. 4 flat or no. 3 round) paint the grout areas around the tiles using the basecoat color (Eggshell or Titanium White) with a little Burnt Umber or Raw Sienna added to make it a little darker than the basecoat. Paint the grout between the tiles also. Then lightly mist the outside edge of the grout with Burnt Umber.

19 If you have "tiled" a tabletop and it will be used heavily, apply several coats of marine spar varnish with a hand brush. This will yellow a bit over time and will add a patina to the tiles, creating a more aged look. If the project will be used for a wall plaque or will not be subject to much surface stress, a waterbased varnish will work well.

Lace Box

This project is both a gift and a gift wrap. It could be a base for decoupage roses and used as a special keepsake by a bride. Line it with wallpaper or fabric for a sewing box. Tuck a gift inside, add a ribbon, and the gift wrap will last forever.

You may use either a wood or a papier-mâché box. As I explain each step I will point out differences between painting on wood and on papier-mâché.

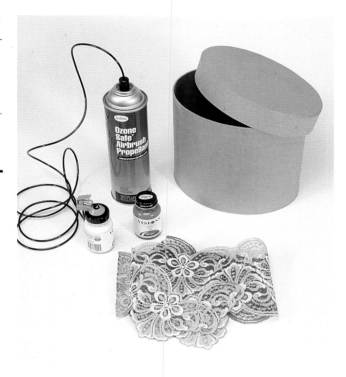

SUPPLIES

- Papier-mâché or wood box (any shape will do)
- Lace, about 2 yards (182.9cm) for the average box
- Visions AirPainter unit (includes canned air and empty bottle)
- Aztek 3000S airbrush
- Visions Opaque colors: White, Teal and Burnt Umber
- Empty bottle for mixing antiquing color
- Repositionable adhesive (not shown)

1 Basecoat the box White with the AirPainter, using a back-and-forth motion around the box and lid. Allow it to dry.
NOTE: I wear a dust mask when I work on a curved surface to avoid breathing in airborne droplets of paint.

2 Add a second coat of White, moving the AirPainter in the opposite direction from the first application to fill the color in as smoothly as possible. On a wood box, you may need to sand between coats to eliminate the raised part of the wood grain and make it smooth for the second coat. If you're using a papier-mâché box, don't load on wet paint too fast. Allow each coat to dry before adding the next. If it gets too wet the surface will begin to sag or release.

3 Spray the smoothest side of the lace with repositionable adhesive and apply the sticky side around the box. Be sure the lace fits all around the bottom edge of the box but does not extend high enough for the image to be obscured by the box lid. Cut two elements out of the lace and position them on the top of the box.

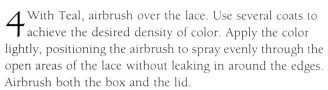

4 With Teal, airbrush over the lace. Use several coats to achieve the desired density of color. Apply the color lightly, positioning the airbrush to spray evenly through the open areas of the lace without leaking in around the edges. Airbrush both the box and the lid.

NOTE: The Aztek 3000S is my choice from this point on for this project. If you use the AirPainter, the spray pattern will be larger but will produce the same effect.

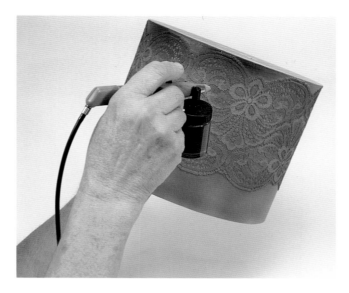

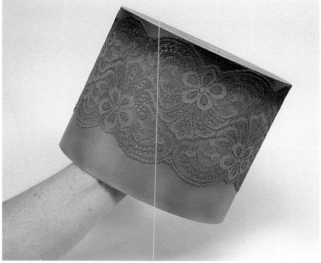

5 Pour some Burnt Umber into your empty bottle. Add Teal a little at a time to create a brownish black color for antiquing. Antique along the bottom edge of the box, allowing the color to fade into the Teal as you move up the box. Allow the paint to dry.

6 Remove the lace carefully. Set it aside to dry thoroughly as it can be used over and over. Put the sticky side on waxed paper to store for another time.

7 Using the antique color you created, lightly spray around the bottom edge of the lace design on the box.

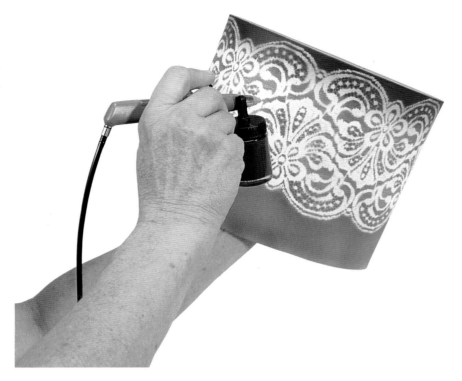

8 Antique around the outside edge of the box lid. Remove the lace and spray a light coat of antiquing over the outside edges of the lace design.

9 Both wood and papier-mâché boxes need a finish coat. You can use a waterbased varnish in your airbrush and seal it with several light coats. After it is thoroughly dry, brush on a final coat of varnish by hand.

Candleglow Cabinet

This is an advanced project for beginners. It looks hard, but it's not. Just take one step at a time and don't rush. The most important skill you need is airbrush control.

I show this design on a small pine cabinet made for me by woodworker Frank Tucker. He copied a primitive and poorly made old cabinet. He just had to smooth and rout the edges, add little button feet and in general "citify" it a bit. The door is flush and as soon as I saw this cabinet, the candle took shape in my mind. This could be done on a black canvas, the back of a wall shelf or on a large pine plaque.

SUPPLIES

- **Pine cabinet (do not attach the door until the very end)**
- **Puritan Pine wood stain by Minwax**
- **ComArt Opaque airbrush colors from the primary colors kit: White Opaque, Light Yellow, Red (or Red Orange), Black; Liquitex Concentrated Artist Colors: Light Gray, Burnt Umber, a strong blue (Swedish Blue or Ultramarine Blue), Silver (optional)**
- **2 sheets of frisket film, matte finish**
- **Felt-tip permanent pen**
- **Cutting knife with a no. 11 blade**

1 Stain the cabinet with Puritan Pine and wipe it down inside and out according to the directions on the Minwax label. Allow it to dry thoroughly, preferably overnight.

2 Place the cabinet door on the easel. Select the side on which the wood grain best reflects or complements the candle design.

3 Trace the candle and holder design onto the frisket with the felt-tip pen. Remove the frisket backing and position the sticky side on the wood surface. Reserve the backing for holding cutouts.

4 Cut around the entire candle and holder and remove the frisket cutout from the wood surface. Place the cutout of the candle and holder on the frisket backing to use later.

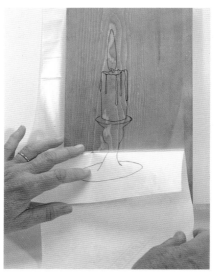

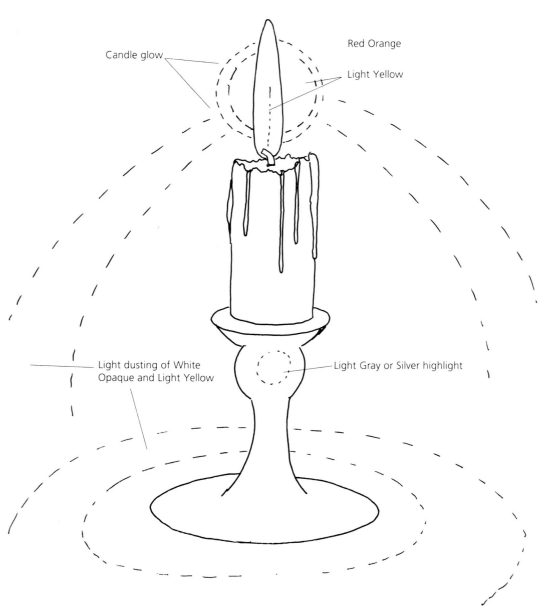

Candle glow

Red Orange

Light Yellow

Light dusting of White Opaque and Light Yellow

Light Gray or Silver highlight

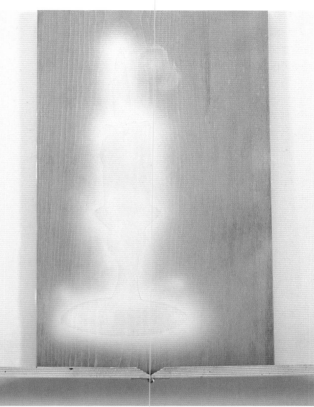

5 With the airbrush 3 to 4½ inches (7.6 to 11.4cm) from the surface, use White Opaque to cover the open candle and holder area. Do this in two or three light coats or until the wood grain no longer shows. Allow the painted area to dry thoroughly.

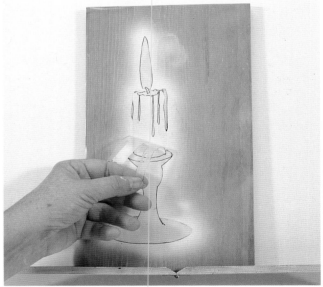

6 Carefully replace the candle cutout into the open painted frisket. Make sure the edges match, and press firmly to re-adhere the frisket.

7 Cut around the main part of the candle and remove it. Leave the drips in place.

8 With Light Yellow in the airbrush, paint a faint band of color across the top edge of candle, allowing it to fade in the candle body.

9 Cut out the top section of the candle, where the wick is located, and remove.

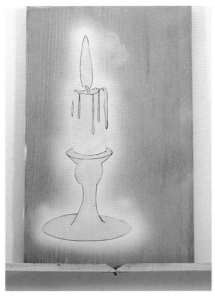

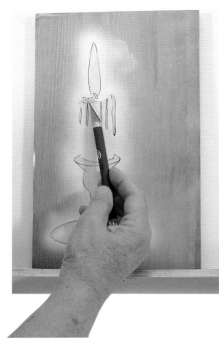

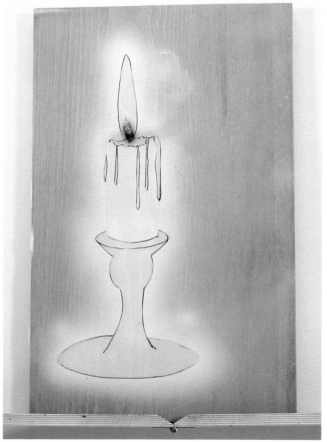

10 Airbrush the top of the candle Yellow, making the color strongest toward the top of the cut. That's the back of the candle top.

11 Carefully cut out the wick and remove it. Airbrush the wick Black.

12 Still using Black, lightly shade the bottom and sides of the candle to create curve and dimension. Very lightly shade along the drips.
NOTE: You can see areas on the frisket where I have checked the airbrush flow and moved in and out of the design. This is part of controlling the airbrush, and only shows on the frisket.

13 Cut the part of the candle holder below the lip. Pull it back, but don't remove it.

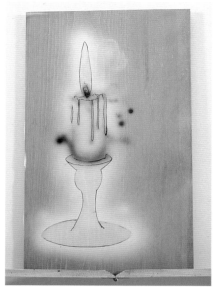

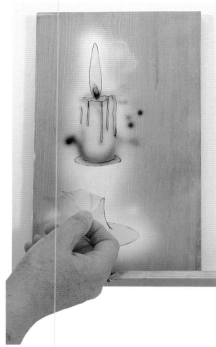

14 Airbrush a black shadow under the lip. Also shade below the ball down to the bottom of the base.

15 Shade the ball area in a circular motion leaving a highlight area in the center.

16 Remove the frisket from the base of the candle holder. Shade the base darkest toward the center, leaving highlights at the edges. Then remove the frisket from the lip.

17 Shade the edge just under the candle to intensify this shadow. NOTE: You can use silver paint to give a metallic look to the candle holder. Add it lightly to the highlight areas on the lip of the candle holder, on the ball part and on the edge of the base.

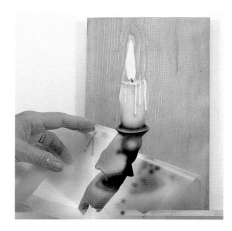

18 Remove all the frisket and allow the painted area to dry. Then re-cover the painted design area with fresh frisket and cut around the candle and holder. Remove the background frisket, leaving the painted candle area masked.

19 Place the door on the cabinet and secure it with hinges outside or tape inside.

20 Add a blue (any strong blue—not a pastel) to Burnt Umber until you get a soft black/brown for shading the background. Leave free of paint an area surrounding the base of the candle holder, and some rays curving from the candle flame. Shade the rest of the background with the mixture you created, airbrushing lightly and deliberately to darken the area all around the candle.

21 With White Opaque in the air-brush create a soft glow over the flame area. Do this by holding your air-brush directly over the candle flame and slowly moving it straight back toward you to widen and soften the spray pattern. Then add a touch of White Opaque at the top of the rays, just out from the candle glow, holding the air-brush about 3 inches (7.6cm) from surface.

22 Leaving the rest of the frisket firmly attached, pull down the flame area to the bottom of the flame. Allow this to hang while you paint the flame.

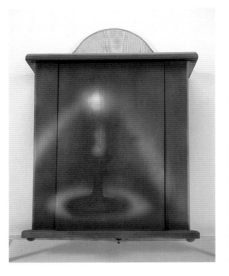 

23 With Red (or Red Orange) in the airbrush add a touch of color at the top of the flame. Also add Red to the wick at the bottom, moving the airbrush toward the center of the flame.

24 When the paint on the flame is dry, replace the flame part of frisket. Holding the airbrush about 2 inches (5.1cm) away from the surface, paint a faint red circle around the outside of the white glow circle.

25 Next add Light Yellow to the glow using a circular motion and fading the color into the flame area.

26 Pull back the flame area of the frisket again and add Yellow to the top of the flame. Add Yellow to the base of the flame at the wick and pull faintly up the center of the flame, stopping at the top of the glow circle.

27 Add a faint bit of Yellow to the highlight at the candle holder base and to the background arcs.

28 Intensify the Yellow color in the center of the flame. Use a light touch and build up color gradually.

29 Remove all the frisket from the surface, pulling it slowly in a downward motion. Review the design. Soften or subdue the shadows if necessary, using the Blue/Burnt Umber mixture.

30 Finally, antique the edges of the cabinet from a 45-degree angle, allowing the color to fade into the center of the wood section. If you have already attached the door, make sure to cover the painted area to avoid overspray.

31 Finish the cabinet by attaching the door if you have not already done so and by adding a small white ceramic knob. Use waterbased varnish thinned to the consistency of 2% milk and lightly mist it on with your airbrush for at least the first coat. After the first coat (to seal and protect the paint) you may apply the varnish with a brush if you like.

A GALLERY OF AIRBRUSH IDEAS

"LOVE LETTERS" QUILT

I entered this quilt in a Quilt Guild contest. The rules required a basic fabric for the theme and some piecing. The pink and blue pieces that are called "flying geese" look like little envelopes when turned upside down. The envelopes and letter writing materials in the large print carried the theme. The Old Fashioned Lady came from the "Great Grandma's Garb" book by Eleanor Zimmerman, and I airbrushed her in a lavender-gray color to look like an old tintype photo. Quilt courtesy of Jim Mossop.

"DUTCH APRONS" QUILT

This is a small 45″×45″ quilt I made for a class in airbrushing for quilters. I used a commercial precut stencil of the tulips in two sizes.

The title of the quilt comes from the red, white and blue fabrics used. The checks, stripes and plaid fabrics come from Holland. When a Dutch lady dresses in her native costume, you can tell the area she is from by the lace cap and the apron she is wearing. I followed the Dutch theme with tulips and apron fabrics my daughter (who lives in Holland) sent me.

DAISY PAIL

This is actually an inexpensive galvanized pail you can find at any hardware store. I washed it and rinsed it in vinegar and water. When it was dry I painted a white basecoat with a metal primer. The eyelet lace trim was attached with magnets and the background was airbrushed around it—light blue first and then a darker blue to blend and shade. The daisies were airbrushed white, the centers yellow and the leaves a basic green. The ladybugs were airbrushed in red with a stencil first, and then with a black overlay for the dots and head. All the detail was done with a liner brush and black acrylic paint. This pail is for my granddaughter Julie's blue-and-daisy bedroom.

CANVAS TOTE BAG

I was hoping to fill this bag with Las Vegas winnings, but I ended up putting my extra shoes in it. The cherry pattern was repeated three times. The area around the cherries was done with masking tape and the line was done with a felt-tip pen. Three cherries usually pays off about three to one. Hope your luck runs better!

"DREAMCATCHER" BY MOLLIE PERRY

Mollie's American Indian heritage shows through in this dreamcatcher she made for me. The design was airbrushed with Liquitex Color Concentrates on a leather chamois, and it hangs from a large stick.

The story of the dreamcatcher is: If you put it near your bed, it catches all the dreams and allows only the pleasant dreams to come through. You will be the dreamer of only good dreams.

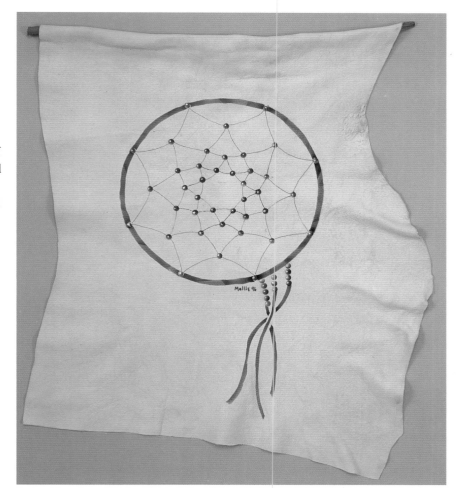

"THE ADORABLES" FROM THE BEADERY

These little plastic boxes come in various shapes and two sizes. They are great for presenting gifts or for holding sewing pins and notions. I used small brass stencils to airbrush the designs with paint from the hobby store that is used on model airplanes. The finish is a model clear coat, and in a gloss returns the original finish over the paint.

The dragon was painted a blue-green color, the stencil was left on and the clear coat was sprayed. The stencil was removed quickly and glitter sprinkled on the surface while the clear coat was still wet. When it was dry another clear coat was added for the finish.

AIRBRUSHED GREETING CARDS

Airbrushing a design on blank greeting cards makes them much more personal. These greeting card blanks are made by Strathmore and come in packages that can be found in craft and stationery stores. The colonial scene is made with a single-layer stencil, and the angel is made with a three-layer stencil. Both stencils are available from American Traditional Stencils.

QUILT SHADOW BOX

This is a small wall shelf that can add an accent in a room. The quilt was painted with an airbrush and a stencil was used. The shadows were lightly painted freehand to give a soft look of draped fabric to the wood. The shelf was stained a pine color and taped off to keep it free of paint. A small plant would look good in the bottom corner, or place a small photo of someone special on the top shelf over the quilt.

ADDRESS NOTEBOOK

This address notebook will hold your holiday card list and keep you up to date. It matches the "Holiday Ornament" photo album project shown on page 70. It was airbrushed on a canvas-covered book in a base color of black.

OUT-OF-THIS-WORLD NOTEBOOK

This notebook is a black canvas-covered book and is easy to paint on. The circles, dot clusters and starbursts can be used anywhere. The entire cover was airbrushed in white. Color can be added here and there to create volume and space gases.

BLACK SILK NECKTIE

I used a Visions Stick-N-Stencil for the images, and metallic fabric dyes in Pearl White and Gold to create the sun and moon theme on this black silk necktie. It's a great look for gals too, with a silk shirt and black velvet skirt.

Product Information/Resources

Aztek Airbrushes; Testor Personal Compressor; Visions AirPainter; Visions Paint; Accu-Flex:
    The Testor Corp.
    620 Buckbee St.
    Rockford IL 61104
    USA

    Testor Canada
    206 Milvan Dr.
    Weston, Ontario, M9L 1Z9
    Canada

    Testor Australia Pty. Ltd.
    34 Keliher
    Darra 4076 Queensland
    Australia

Liquitex Concentrated Artist Colors; Acrylic Wood Stains; Flow-Aid:
    Binney & Smith Inc.
    1100 Church Lane
    P.O. Box 431
    Easton PA 18044-0431
    USA

Liquitex International:
    Binney & Smith (Canada) Ltd.
    Toronto Sales and Distribution
      Office
    40 East Pearce St.
    Richmond Hill, Ontario,
      Canada
    L4B 1B7

    Binney & Smith (Europe) Ltd.
    Amphill Road
    Bedford MK42 9RS
    England

    Binney & Smith (Australia) Ltd.
    599 Blackburn Rd.
    Clayton North 3168
    P.O. Box 684
    Glen Waverly 3150 Victoria,
      Australia

Jo Sonja Artist Colors:
    Chroma Acrylics, Inc.
    905 Bucky Dr.
    Lititz PA 17543
    USA

    Chroma Acrylics Australia
      (N.S.W.) Pty. Ltd.
    P.O. Box 3 B
    Mt. Kuring, GAI N.S.W. 2080
    Australia

ComArt Opaque Primary Color Set and ComArt Transparent Primary Color Set; Eclipse Airbrush by Iwata:
    Medea
    P.O. Box 14397
    Portland OR 97214
    USA

American Traditional Stencils (English Ivy; Heart and Ribbons):
    The Stencil Outlet
    P.O. Box 80
    West Nottingham NH 03261
    USA
    Phone 800-2-STENCIL to
      request catalog

Wooden signboards and boxes:
    Walnut Hollow Farm
    1409 State Rd. 23
    Dodgeville WI 53533
    USA

Rustic pine cabinet for "Candleglow Cabinet" and pegged board for "Heart and Ribbons":
    Frank Tucker, Woodworker
    13345 Deerwood Rd.
    Apple Valley CA 92308
    USA

Canvas-covered paintable items ("Holiday Ornament" photo album):
    The Dalee Book Co.
    129 Clinton Place
    Yonkers NY 10701
    USA

Dalee Book Co. Distributors in Japan:
    Sun-K
    1-11-15 Higashi-Nihondahai
      Chu-O-KU
    Tokyo-103
    Japan

    Setoco, Inc.
    3-27-10 Chikusa, Chikusa-Ku
    Nagoya 464
    Japan

    Dalee Book Co. Distributors in
      Australia:
    Timber Turn Pty. Ltd.
    1-3 Shepley Ave.
    Panorama 5041
    So. Australia

The following products can be found at your local art supply, craft, model and hobby, tole painting or hardware stores:
    The Beadery/Adorables: small
      plastic boxes with lids
    Designs by Bentwood:
      bentwood boxes with lids
    Duralene by Seth Cole: stencil
      film
    Original Frisket by Frisk
    Pactra Enamels
    Royal Garden Brushes by Royal
      Brush Co.
    The Tracer projector by
      Artograph
    W.N. Wonder & Co., Inc.:
      crackle medium

Index

More Great Books
for Creating Beautiful Crafts!

The Decorative Painting Color Match Sourcebook—Take the guesswork out of your painting with this innovative guide to simple, proven formulas for mixing and matching colors. You'll be able to cross-match colors among all the major paint brands: Accent, Americana, Ceramcoat, Folk Art, Jo Sonja and Liquitex! #30976/$19.99/96 pages/360 color swatches/paperback

1,200 Paint Effects for the Home Decorator—Now you can find the ideal color combination and paint effect for any kind of job! This handy visual guide gives you over 1,200 combinations, based on 25 standard colors. Plus, step-by-step instructions for special finishing effects such as splattering, combing, color washing, marbling, distressing and more! #30949/$29.99/192 pages/1,000+ color illus.

Acrylic Decorative Painting Techniques—Discover stroke-by-stroke instruction that takes you through the basics and beyond! More than 50 fun and easy painting techniques are illustrated in simple demonstrations that offer at least two variations on each method. Plus, a thorough discussion on tools, materials, color, preparation and backgrounds. #30884/$24.99/128 pages/550 color illus.

Making Greeting Cards With Rubber Stamps—Discover hundreds of quick, creative, stamp-happy ways to make extra-special cards—no experience, fancy equipment or expensive materials required! You'll find 30 easy-to-follow projects for holidays, birthdays, thank you's and more! #30821/$21.99/128 pages/231 color illus./paperback

The Crafter's Guide to Pricing Your Work—Price and sell more than 75 kinds of crafts with this must-have reference. You'll learn how to set prices to maximize income while maintaining a fair profit margin. Includes tips on record-keeping, consignment, taxes, reducing costs and managing your cash flow. #70353/$16.99/160 pages/paperback

The Decorative Stamping Sourcebook—Embellish walls, furniture, fabric and accessories—with stamped designs! You'll find 180 original, traceable motifs in a range of themes and illustrated instructions for making your own stamps to enhance any decorating style. #30898/$24.99/128 pages/200 color illus.

Decorative Painting Sourcebook—Priscilla Hauser, Phillip Myer and Jackie Shaw lend their expertise to this one-of-a-kind guide straight from the pages of *Decorative Artist's Workbook*! You'll find step-by-step, illustrated instructions on every technique—from basic brushstrokes to faux finishes, painting glassware, wood, clothing and much more! #30883/$24.99/128 pages/200 color illus./paperback

Painting & Decorating Birdhouses—Turn unfinished birdhouses into something special—from a quaint Victorian roost to a Southwest pueblo, from a rustic log cabin to a lighthouse! These colorful and easy decorative painting projects are for the birds with 22 clever projects to create indoor decorative birdhouses, as well as functional ones to grace your garden. #30882/$23.99/128 pages/194 color illus./paperback

Painting Houses, Cottages and Towns on Rocks—Discover how a dash of paint can turn humble stones into charming cottages, churches, Victorian mansions and more. This hands-on, easy-to-follow book offers a menagerie of fun—and potentially profitable—stone animal projects. Eleven examples, complete with material lists, photos of the finished piece and patterns will help you create entire rock villages. #30823/$21.99/128 pages/398 color illus./paperback

Airbrush Artist's Pocket Palette—This handy reference shows you how to achieve the effects and textures you're after—saving time, frustration and materials. #30835/$17.99/64 pages/400+ color illus.

Creative Paint Finishes for Furniture—Revive your furniture with fresh color and design! Inexpensive, easy and fun painting techniques are at your fingertips, along with step-by-step directions and a photo gallery of imaginative applications for *faux* finishing, staining, stenciling, mosaic, découpage and many other techniques. #30748/$27.99/144 pages/236 color, 7 b&w illus.

The Art of Painting Animals on Rocks—Discover how a dash of paint can turn humble stones into charming "pet rocks." This hands-on easy-to-follow book offers a menagerie of fun—and potentially profitable—stone animal projects. Eleven examples, complete with material lists, photos of the finished piece and patterns will help you create a forest of fawns, rabbits, foxes and other adorable critters. #30606/$21.99/144 pages/250 color illus./paperback

Dynamic Airbrush—In this visually exciting book, 2 professional, award-winning airbrush illustrators take readers through a series of challenging airbrush projects. #30765/$24.99/176 pages/300 color, 30 b&w illus/paperback

Creative Paint Finishes for the Home—A complete, full-color, step-by-step guide to decorating floors, walls and furniture—including how to use the tools, master the techniques and develop ideas. #30426/$27.99/144 pages/212 color illus.

Airbrush Action 4—Looking for ideas and inspiration? Just open this volume which showcases the best new work created by airbrush artists. You'll uncover hundreds of images from today's leading artists, including Coula, Fredrickson, Mayer and Steirnagle! #30781/$29.99/192 pages/400+ color illus./paperback

Everything You Ever Wanted to Know About Fabric Painting—Discover how to create beautiful fabrics! You'll learn how to set up workspace, choose materials, plus the ins and outs of tie-dye, screen printing, woodgraining, marbling, cyanotype and more! #30625/$21.99/128 pages/4-color throughout/paperback

Paint Craft—Discover great ideas for enhancing your home, wardrobe and personal items. You'll see how to master the basics of mixing and planning colors, how to print with screen and linoleum to create your own stationery, how to enhance old glassware and pottery pieces with unique patterns and motifs and much more! #30678/$16.95/144 pages/200 color illus./paperback

Basic Airbrush Painting Techniques—Blow a breath of fresh air into your creative life by learning the art of airbrushing with Judy Martin! You'll develop your control of the airbrush and learn new techniques such as masking, producing surface effects, correcting and retouching to make your artwork shine! #30570/$19.95/128 pages/230 color illus./paperback

How to Airbrush T-Shirts and Other Clothing—Make a statement and a buck by painting T-shirts and other garments with 18 step-by-step demonstrations that teach all the basic-level techniques you'll need. You'll discover how to transfer illustrations onto a garment, create designs freehand or with stencils, work on different fabrics, produce textures and much more. #30614/$24.99/128 pages/200+ color, 15 b&w illus./paperback

Other fine North Light Books are available from your local bookstore, art supply store, or direct from the publisher. Write to the address below for a FREE catalog of all North Light Books. To order books directly from the publisher, include $3.50 postage and handling for one book, $1.50 for each additional book. Ohio residents add 6% sales tax. Allow 30 days for delivery.

North Light Books
1507 Dana Avenue
Cincinnati, Ohio 45207

VISA/MasterCard orders call TOLL-FREE
1-800-289-0963

Prices subject to change without notice.   Stock may be limited on some books.

Write to this address for information on *The Artist's Magazine*, North Light Books, North Light Book Club, Graphic Design Book Club, North Light Art School, and Betterway Books. To receive information on art or design competitions, send a SASE to Dept. BOI, Attn: Competition Coordinator, at the above address.

8548